COLORS O̶ ̶̶̶̶̶̶̶̶ATION

substance abuse

By
Brad Duncan

Bradleyjeep Publishing
ISBN #978-1-949908-00-8

Cover art by Jennifer Legate
Copyright 2020

Dedicated to Justin Watson.

*Although your life on earth was brief,
your impact was mighty.*

About Colors of Salvation

On January 11th, 1866, Pastor Charles Spurgeon, in a message to orphan children, shared the verse from Psalm 51:7b "Wash me, and I shall be whiter than snow." He used this verse and some basic colors to share the good news of the gospel of Jesus.[1]

Later, the Colors of Salvation booklet was created. It is a wordless booklet used to share the gospel. A variety of colors have been used through the years as symbols for these steps of a Christian's spiritual life. I have chosen to use the following colors for this publication:

[Gray]
Gray represents the color of ashes. "Ashes to ashes; dust to dust" is a common phrase used at funerals. This color symbolizes death and the sinful state of all people before God. (Genesis 3:19b)

[Red]
Red represents the saving blood of Jesus. (1 John 1:7)

[White]
White represents the perfect righteousness God gives to a believer through faith in Jesus. (Psalm 51:7)

[Blue]
Blue represents a believer's baptism. (Acts 2:38)

[Green]
Green represents growth in the Christian faith. (Colossians 2:6-7)

[Gold]
Gold represents a believer's eternal home in heaven. (Revelation 21:21-22)

[Final Thoughts]
I have also included a section at the end of each story allowing each person to emphasize their final thoughts.

Inspiration for this Book

On a hot summer day, my mind wandered as I stood in a long receiving line overflowing from a funeral home. I was there to pay my respects to my family members who had lost their 21 year-old son to a drug overdose. Seeing and feeling the hurt from this deadly epidemic, I wondered if there was something I could do. I asked God if He could use me in some way to help in this fight. He inspired me to share hope — the hope found in the power of Jesus to not only overcome this epidemic, but our ultimate need of conquering sin. This book contains true stories of those who have fought this battle and overcome it by the power of Jesus.

I am humbled to tell the stories of these incredible people. I've been shocked, saddened, elated, and filled with hope through reading the events of their lives. It's an honor to share them with you.

Substance abuse is found in every area of our society. It respects no boundaries. This being the case, I have intentionally included a variety of ages, races, genders, and social statuses in these pages.

I also feel led by God to give a portion of the proceeds from this book to ministries and charities who are fighting substance abuse and helping people with recovery.

Finally, if you have a problem with substance abuse or have a friend or family member who does, my prayer is that you find hope in the stories shared in the following pages. Jesus offers hope and healing to all who seek Him. These are the true stories of real people who are fighting the good fight of faith!

Neil's Story

[Gray]

I grew up in a loving, middle class family. My dad coached me and my older brother in sports growing up, and my mom was always at our games. I was a pretty good kid and made good grades. As a teenager I did a few dumb things like drinking alcohol on the weekends sometimes but never anything I considered really bad. I'd seen friends of mine mess up their lives with drugs and partying, and that wasn't going to be me. I had big plans for my future.

Everything changed during a high school basketball game when I was 18. A collision caused me to herniate a disc in my lower back. Surgery soon followed. Waking up in the recovery room, I distinctly remember having a morphine drip in my arm. I was immediately in love!

Shortly after my surgery I moved away from home for my freshman year of college. They had prescribed me a bottle of ninety 10 mg hydrocodone pills. At the bottom of that bottle it said "unlimited refills". I put that claim to the test. Sure enough, in my first month in college, I refilled that bottle five times in a single week at the same pharmacy. No one batted an eye.

After four years of convincing my doctor I still needed the drugs, he finally cut me off. This was the first time in my life I had felt true despair. A friend of mine worked at a pharmacy, and we worked out a deal to keep the drugs flowing. This worked for a couple of years until the DEA busted him. I found out I was on their radar too. After hiding out for a couple of weeks, I became violently ill from the withdrawals. I remember during that episode praying for the first time in years. I told God that if he would keep me out of jail, then I'd give up the drugs and get my act together.

Amazingly, after some miraculous turn of events, the DEA stopped pursuing me. Of course I didn't keep my end of the bargain with God. My drug use escalated out of control. A few years later I married the love of my life, and unfortunately for her, drugs were more important than our marriage. We went on a cruise for our honeymoon. I couldn't get enough drugs for the trip, so I went through opiate withdrawals the entire time. I was miserable, and I didn't try to hide it. I ruined our honeymoon. That

11

was just a sample of what the next five years of her life would be like. I was a thief, a liar, a manipulator — a junky, plain and simple.

Life as an addict became miserable. During the last two or three months of my addiction, I began actively trying to kill myself. Even though I had a wonderful wife, very young twins, and friends and family who loved me dearly, life still felt empty and hopeless. I had tried everything to get off the drugs — Narcotics Anonymous, doctors, other 12-step programs — the whole routine. Nothing worked.

I became infatuated with death. By this time, I had watched many of my buddies fall dead all around me, and I wanted that too. Several times a day I would shoot up combinations of drugs that should never be combined. But as much as I tried, for some reason, my heart wouldn't stop beating. I thought everyone I loved would be better off without me, and the sooner I died the better for everyone. It was at this point God gave me one of the greatest gifts I had ever received: a jail cell.

[Red]

I was arrested for shoplifting. Although my family saw it as a cry for help, my wife, Rebekah, saw it as the last straw. She said if I went to rehab she would give me one last chance, but we both knew it wasn't going to work. My family helped me find a court approved alternative called the Renewal Ranch. I had no desire to go there, not because I didn't want to get better, but because I didn't believe there was any hope of me getting better.

Once at the ranch, the pastors there began sharing truth from the Bible with me. I had grown up in church, but in college I had a very influential philosophy teacher who gave me an easy out. He argued there was no heaven or hell, no God to answer to. And I liked the idea. It was easier to desire death and the peace it would bring if there was no afterlife, no consequences for my actions.

Apparently God wasn't as comfortable with the idea. He kept pursuing me. My heart wasn't opened by cold theological arguments but by warm personal encounters. The first encounters, which started to break the walls down around my hardened heart, were with the other men at the ranch. They didn't know me, but they comforted, loved, and prayed for me right from the start. Defensively I would think, "What kind of cult have I gotten myself into?" But it was the love of Jesus coming from these real men —

who had experienced much of what I had experienced — that got me to a place where I could have my second encounter.

We had to memorize a lot of Bible verses as part of the curriculum at the ranch. On my third day there, I dropped some papers. As I bent over to pick them up, a Bible verse grabbed my attention. It was Jeremiah 33:3, "Call to me and I will answer you, and will tell you great and hidden things that you have not known." I remember rolling my eyes and thinking, "You'll answer me, huh?"

[White]

Later that evening, I was laying wide awake for the third straight night in a row on a couch in the main house. I laid there broken, scared, and ashamed. I guess I had finally slowed down enough to have a chance to stop and think about what I had done with my life, what I had done to the people I loved, and the mess I had made of everything — how my 18 month-old twins wouldn't have their daddy around for the next six months of their lives. As I laid there, shaking and crying, I felt like I was having a panic attack. I didn't know what to do, so I decided to take God up on the promise he made me in that verse I read earlier.

I started to pray for the first time in a long, long time. I said, "God if you're real, if you have something better planned for my life, if you have something else for me, then I need to know, because I can't do this anymore." I became broken and remember saying "I'm sorry" over and over and over.

It was as if the lights came on, like I wasn't in the dark anymore. An overwhelming sense of peace came over me that I knew I didn't deserve. In that moment I felt like God was right there with me. As I laid there, I prayed and confessed everything I could think of to confess. And I just talked to God. It was almost like I was catching up with an old friend who had been there all along, but I hadn't realized it. I felt him there with me. By the time the sun came up the next morning, he had taken away all of the shame, embarrassment, and guilt which had been suffocating me for so long.

This was my first encounter with Jesus Christ. It changed me. Not all at once, but it began something in me that hasn't slowed down even a little since it happened. I finally found the truth that I never knew I was missing. I wasn't even looking for it, but God was looking for me.

[Blue]

I believe my baptism was part of God's perfect timing. I have never felt as much clear direction from God over anything as much as my baptism. After being freed from addiction and death, I felt compelled to be obedient to God's Word and to be publicly baptized.

My wife, Rebekah, and I decided to be baptized together. She had never been baptized, although she's followed Christ since she was a kid. Her mom, who always set an amazing example of how to live a faith-filled life, had led her to Jesus at an early age.

Unfortunately, a few months before we were baptized, her mom was diagnosed with a rare form of breast cancer. She had always wanted to see Rebekah get baptized. So, in God's timing, her mom got to see her daughter and son-in-law baptized a couple of months before she went to be with Jesus herself.

[Green]

I graduated from Renewal Ranch in June of 2018. I'm still trying to learn as much as I can about being a follower of Jesus. I'm steadily trying to learn to rely on God's strength and not my own. It's definitely a process.

God took a lying, thieving, manipulative junky on the verge of death and breathed new life into me. He changed me from the inside out. He's changing me still. God is restoring me.

Rebekah had become hopeless about our marriage. However, over the last year and a half, God has completely restored our relationship. I can honestly say that she is my best friend, and we've never been closer.

My parents have gone from being unable to trust me to being proud of me. My kids have gone from living without a father to having a godly father raising them in the Lord and leading them by example.

Recently, I found out about an addiction ministry my friend was heading up at my church. I chose to serve there for one reason: I want to see God at work! I've experienced the saving power of Jesus Christ myself and witnessed him change the lives of many other men while at the Renewal Ranch. I don't ever want to stop being part of his work while I'm on this earth.

[Gold]

The idea of an everlasting life became one of the biggest barriers to me wanting to believe in God. Before my salvation, life was exhausting. Because of this, I had tried to end my life several times. The thought of a never-ending life sounded more like torture than a reward. Before I experienced Jesus, all I knew was darkness. I woke up every morning with dread in my heart for whatever the day was about to bring. Who in their right mind would want that to go on forever?

But Jesus changes everything. Once I learned of His grace and tasted the abundant life He offers, I realized He has actually placed eternity in our hearts. One of the most powerful truths I've learned is that God is faithful. He can be trusted. So I believe it when He says, "No eye has seen, no ear has heard, and no mind has imagined what God has prepared for those who love him." (1 Corinthians 2:9)

Although I have had friends and family who had faith in Jesus die from disease and overdose, I know God can be trusted. I will not grieve like those who have no hope. My hope is in the Lord Jesus Christ.

[Final Thoughts]

Despite the lies I used to tell myself, I now understand there is nothing in my past that Jesus can't forgive. And once you believe it, once you receive it, once you know Him, you'll know how good He is. And once you know in your heart you've been forgiven, you start living differently. You live grateful for the grace you've been given. And the grace of Jesus changes everything.

words of [HOPE]

"The Lord says, "I will rescue those who love me.
I will protect those who trust in my name.
When they call on me, I will answer;
I will be with them in trouble.
I will rescue and honor them."
Psalm 91:14-15

The number of people who have been impacted by substance abuse is overwhelming. We've all heard the stories of popular athletes, movie stars, and famous personalities who have struggled with addiction. Most of us know someone personally who has struggled with this issue. I've had family members and friends who have battled substance abuse. Some are winning their fight and are living in day-to-day victory. Others have succumbed and gone into eternity. This book is filled with true stories of people who have fought substance abuse, been saved through the blood of Jesus Christ, and are now boldly living for Jesus! May their stories of God's grace fill you with the hope of Jesus!

Brad Duncan

Kathy's Story

[Gray]

Growing up as the youngest of four children in my dad's home wasn't easy. A revolving number of stepmoms was very confusing for a young girl and usually led to me feeling like a burden. Abandonment, depression, and self-esteem issues were prevalent in my formative years.

I wasn't raised going to church, but I did go every so often with my friends. The only thing I knew about the Bible is we had one open on our coffee table as a decoration. It simply gathered dust and nicotine. The powerful, life-changing words contained within it were never shared with me.

My dad's relationships usually consisted of arguing, yelling, and fighting with his spouse or girlfriend. Miraculously, the few times I went to church with friends planted a seed, and when I was scared in the midst of the chaos at home, I would cry out to God. He gave me peace.

When I was 10 years old I got to take a friend camping with my family. We were in the camper complaining about my parents cigarette smoke burning our eyes, so my stepmom gave us each a cup of whiskey and coke to knock us out. We didn't like the taste, but I loved the feeling it gave me.

On that night, I began my relationship with alcohol. It became routine for me to sneak around and steal it from my dad's liquor cabinet. By the age of 15, drinking and smoking with my dad was common.

As a teenager, I always felt like an outcast — unloved and unwanted. But drinking took all of those bad feelings away. I even started hanging out with the cheerleaders and popular people at school, but I still didn't feel like I was really part of the cool crowd. Tragically, one of those cheerleaders, who was so beautiful and full of love, died in a drinking and driving accident on her 14th birthday. What should have been a wake-up call for me, wasn't. In fact, my drinking only got worse.

Later on, in my early 20's, I got married. I quit drinking around my husband. My drunkenness was uncomfortable for him, because his family didn't drink or smoke. I agreed to abstain but would still sneak around and get drunk when he was out of town.

At the age of 24, I was diagnosed with non-systemic lupus disease. At 25, I became pregnant. I felt wonderful the entire pregnancy.

Unfortunately, after I gave birth, my lupus went full blown systemic, and I became very sick. The anti-inflammatory medicine was too hard on my digestive system, so they put me on narcotics. I loved how the narcotics took away the pain and gave me energy to get out of bed. Before long I was taking more than prescribed and eventually ended up in a methadone clinic.

For the next 20 years, I was in and out of Alcoholics Anonymous. I did just enough to pacify my sponsors, not realizing I was only hurting myself by not engaging in the process. Over time, depression and despair overwhelmed me, and I became suicidal.

[Red]
God showed himself faithful throughout my life by allowing friends to plant seeds of truth into me. At an early age, I believed there was a God, but I didn't embrace His salvation until I was 32 years old.

[White]
I had been sober for a short time, but still felt a big void inside of me. I knew something was missing, so my husband and I started going to church. I knew that's what I had been missing all along and went to talk to Rick Grant at First Baptist Church of Benton. He explained God's love and salvation to me. I accepted Jesus, but my seed was planted in shallow soil, because I wasn't in the word of God.

[Blue]
My baptism was a special event, and I was happy to be known as God's child. However, I didn't realize how hard following Jesus and conquering my addictions would be.

[Green]
After someone is saved you would expect them to just grow in godliness and steadily move away from sin. My experience wasn't like this at all. Although I knew I was saved, my addictions became worse. I didn't get into the power of God's Word. I was trying to live life in my own power. I believe that's why relapsing was worse for me.

I increased my drinking, using narcotics, and escalated to smoking crack. My dope dealers were local gang members who I hung out with. At times, I would even take my son, who I loved, right into the middle of the danger. Other times, I would disappear from home and drift from place to place.

Most people gave me no hope. It got so bad, one drug dealer tried to convince me to see what I was doing to myself. He pointed out how much weight I had lost and said I needed to go home. This didn't convince me to stop. I still chose my addiction.

I watched so many women get beaten up and treated horribly. It still amazes me that I never had a hand laid on me. God had His hedge of protection around me, even in the midst of my addiction, while I was running from Him.

Over the next few years things remained chaotic. I tried to kill myself again, was in and out of mental hospitals, and had multiple drunk driving accidents. Fortunately, I never hurt anyone.

But God continued to pursue me. In 2014 I was bragging on my son for helping a homeless man. He told me to stop telling everyone about what he had done, because of what God's word says about helping others. He opened the Bible to Matthew for me to read. It was in Matthew 6, "Do not do good things so that people will see you do them. If you do, you will get no reward from your Father in heaven." As I looked over to the left, my eyes landed on Matthew 5:36-37 which says, "Nor shall you make an oath by your head, for you cannot make one hair white or black. But let your statement be, 'Yes, yes' or 'No, no'; anything beyond these is of evil."

Wow! Just about everything I said in those days were lies, but I would swear I was telling the truth. This caught my full attention and I thought to myself, "I wonder what else is in here I need to know?" Mind you, I was on 18 different meds, popping narcotics and tranquilizers, and smoking cigarettes while reading God's Word. Thankfully, God doesn't say, "Clean up first and then come to me." But He says, "Come to me as you are, so that I can change you!" I could never stop the drugs on my own. It was only through the power of Jesus I could ever be set free.

Satan made another hard run at me, throwing my wicked past at me. In desperation, I opened my Bible, and in that glorious moment God revealed Psalm 119:71 to me, "It was good for me that I was afflicted, that I may learn your statutes." Through those words, freedom rang out, and I was set free!

The enemy couldn't hold my past against me any longer. Every time he tried to bring up my past, I would start quoting that scripture out loud and thanking God for it all. It didn't matter where I was, I would speak that verse out loud. Believe me, I got some looks, but I didn't care. My life was at stake, and I knew God was the only one who could save me.

The doctors had said I would never be able to work again, but God said, "Yes you can!" and I did! I was only three months sober when I went to work at a church daycare, cooking for a bunch of God's precious children. I was excited, so I called my son, who didn't think I was a particularly good cook, to tell him I got a job. He asked me where the job was, and when I told him he said, "Oh, those poor little children!"

That job is where I really learned to listen to the Holy Spirit, and I want you to know those children and adults loved my cooking! I worked there for a little over two years and I loved it. It was amazing, because I was never able to keep a job longer than two months during my active addiction.

Life has dealt me blessings and disappointments since being set free from my drug and alcohol addiction. After getting my driver's license back, some loving Christian people donated a car to me. My relationship with my son and family is healing and getting better. On the other hand, I've experienced losing my brother to cancer and even some pain in church relationships. But through it all, I've stayed sober and learned to keep my eyes on Jesus. God gives me peace, and I don't feel a need to numb the pain, but to embrace it as I grow through it.

God's timing is always perfect, and He is always right on time. He knows what's best for me, and He places people in my life to help guide me, support me, pray for me, encourage me, and hold me accountable in my walk with Him. It's wonderful to not have to go through life alone.

In July of 2018, I met Cecilee, who is the sweetest child of God I've ever known. She invited me to Regen, a Christian ministry focused on helping people overcome anything coming between them and God. They accepted me with love and invited me back. I thought this would just help me maintain my recovery, but it turned out to be so much more.

Regen helped me dig deeper into God's Word, and taught me who I am in Jesus. It held me accountable in my recovery, helped me to serve others, and to build relationships with other believers. Our Regen community allows us to love, pray, and encourage one another.

The love I felt from my new Regen family when my brother passed away was overwhelming. They called, sent cards and flowers, prayed for me, encouraged me, and reminded me I didn't have to go through my loss alone.

[Gold]

I believe heaven will be a place where there will be no more tears or pain. We'll be dancing on streets paved in gold and singing with the angels. There will always be a feast available at the table of the Lord. Most of all, we'll literally be with Jesus Christ! Oh what a glorious day that will be!

I know I must be here until Jesus calls me home. I must stay and serve others. Jesus wants me to show others His love, but I do look forward to that beautiful new life in heaven above.

[Final Thoughts]

I now serve as a co-leader in a step group, and I absolutely love it. I'm blessed to be a small part of something so amazing. I'll never take the grace of God for granted. I'm so undeserving of the love of Jesus, but He loves me anyway. Oh what a Savior!

words of [WISDOM]

2018 data shows that every day 128 people in the United States die after overdosing on opioids. That's over 46,000 people a year. [2]

"It's gonna get harder before it gets easier. But it will get better. You just gotta make it through the hard stuff first."
-Anonymous

Roughly 25 percent of patients who are prescribed opioids for chronic pain misuse them. [2]

Jason's Story

[Gray]

I was born in Independence, Missouri. I had a great family, a loving mother, a hard working father, and two older brothers who I looked up to. We went to church regularly.

It was a struggle for me to fit in and feel accepted, even in my own family, because of my extreme ADHD. The medicine they used back then turned me into a zombie, so my parents took me off of it. School, church, and even family members didn't know how to deal with me. As a child I took it to heart when people continually said I was a bad kid who wouldn't amount to anything.

At about 10 years old I started hanging out with the wrong crowd, because they accepted me. Smoking cigarettes was the start of a lot of bad decisions for me. I also began using weed and soon needed a way to pay for my bad habits. Stealing from my parents and eventually breaking into cars became my way of paying for them.

My neighbor, Missy, accepted me completely. At 12 years old she was my best friend, and we talked about everything. At that point in my life, she was one of my few positive influences. She meant the world to me. Tragically, in the summer of 1992 Missy drowned in her swimming pool. I can still feel the heartache of the moment when I heard the news. This brought on more pain, depression, and feelings I didn't know how to handle. She loved Jesus, and I couldn't understand how this could happen. I was mad at everyone, including God.

Shortly after her death, alcohol entered my life. Mixing weed with alcohol was my way of escaping the pain. Living numb was better than experiencing the immense pain I was feeling. At 14, I was angry to find out my dad took a new job as a supervisor with his company in another town. It was traumatic to up and leave everything I ever knew, and I didn't handle it very well. Quickly finding the wrong crowd again, I increased my alcohol and drug use, adding meth, acid, and random pills to the rotation. I also began jumping from one unhealthy relationship to another with girls. Stealing from my parents increased, and I began selling drugs to support my habits. My relationship with my parents continued to deteriorate, but I didn't care.

A new girl entered my life who was as wild and crazy as me. At 19 years old, I found out she was pregnant with my son. I tried to straighten up for a while, but once he was born, my life went downhill. I ended up getting in trouble with the law and spending time in and out of jail over the next couple of years. After finding out she had been unfaithful to me while I was in jail, we broke up. With deep regret, I also handed my son over to my parents. I realized I couldn't manage my own life, and I was in no shape to be a father. I basically lost everything.

I moved to Kansas City and continued to abuse alcohol and drugs, ending up back in jail. Once released, I got a job at KFC and met the girl who would become the love of my life. We moved back to Independence so she could attend college. We were happy to find out she was pregnant and looked forward to having our first child together. Unfortunately, I ended up getting another probation violation which led to me going to prison this time. This hit me hard emotionally. I had been doing pretty good and had just found out we were going to have a son. Now everything was being taken away from me, yet again.

While in prison I found out I had another child. The mother of my oldest child had gotten pregnant just before we broke up. I feared telling my wife, but I knew I couldn't hide it from her. I thought for sure she would leave me, and I would lose everything again, but she didn't. She never gave up on me, coming to visit and encourage me throughout my prison sentence. Thankfully, I was released from prison the day before our son was born.

After leaving prison, I walked the straight and narrow road for a little while, but soon reverted back to drinking. After a long court battle, we got custody of my other sons. So within three years, we went from having no kids living with us to having four kids in our home. I was trying to be a dad, a husband, and hold down a job, but my addictions were causing me to fail. My wife and I fought all the time. Just getting through each day was a struggle.

Over the next couple of years I kept making bad decisions and served some time in jail again. After my release we reached our breaking point, separated, and filed for divorce. On the day before we were set to finalize our divorce, she showed up to ask if we could talk. We agreed to start fresh, take things slow, and try to mend our marriage. I knew in my heart I truly loved her and wanted to be with her. Our divorce was avoided.

As time went on, we had our ups and downs, and I was in and out of jail a few more times. We had another child, giving us a total of five kids now. We began going to church living what I would call the American Christian life - attending church but still living like the world.

I had no happiness anymore, and there wasn't any joy in my life due to my addictions. I weighed the most I had ever weighed, and my health was the worst it had ever been. Every negative thing ever said about me was ringing true in my mind. I believed I was a bad person, I would never amount to anything, and I would never truly be accepted by anyone.

[Red]

I had talked to people in church before about my problems, but this time I was completely honest with my friend, Kevin, who was a pastor on staff at our church. He was starting a Celebrate Recovery program and asked me to commit to showing up one night a week.

I agreed and went home to tell my wife. I didn't think she would believe me, because I had lied to her and let her down so many times before. In an amazing extension of grace, she not only supported me, but agreed to attend with me.

Although I showed up for the meetings, I wouldn't remain sober for more than a day or two. My wife and friends didn't give up on me, even though I felt like giving up on myself. They showed me the love of Jesus. After some rather epic binges, I went to church one Sunday morning unaware God had a divine appointment planned for me that day.

[White]

This particular Sunday, Pastor Kevin was preaching on how it's impossible to walk with God without feeling conviction when we sin. At the end of the service the weight of the world came down on me, and I knew I needed to go to the altar. I don't remember walking up the aisle, but as I knelt down the conviction of all my sins came down on me like never before. I was sobbing like a baby as my body was trembling from immense conviction. I was sweating, crying, shaking, and felt like I was being crushed. I couldn't form any thoughts of my own, but I could distinctly hear one voice cutting through all the confusion speaking to my soul.

Later, after searching the Scriptures, I realized that voice was revealing the truth of Romans 8:27-28, "And he who searches our hearts knows the mind of the Spirit, because the Spirit intercedes for God's people in accordance with the will of God. And we know that in all things God works for the good of those who love him, who have been called according to his purpose."

Pastor Kevin walked over, put his arm around me, and prayed for me. When I stood up, I was a new man. All of my pain, hurt, and regret was gone. At the altar, Jesus saved me. He did what I could never do on my own, breaking the chains of my addiction and redeeming my soul. He gave me a new life and a new heart.

[Blue]

I had a complete life change. Reading the Bible, enjoying church activities, and transforming into a healthy husband and father was refreshing. But something inside of me still felt off. Through prayer and reading my Bible, I realized my baptism earlier in life wasn't as a true believer. Others were getting baptized at the time, so I did too. As I like to say now, I just got wet.

I wanted to get my baptism on the right side of my salvation, and I knew without a doubt this was what the Lord was telling me. After speaking with my pastor, my heart was full when my wife decided to be baptized along with me. So, we were baptized together in front of our entire church family. It was amazing to be able to share this moment with my wife.

As I was immersed beneath the water, I focused on the death of my sins and rising from the water's depths. I felt completely renewed. I watched tearfully as my wife was baptized next, and we both stood there afterwards crying happy tears and hugging one another.

[Green]

Since the day of my salvation I have had this fire, this hunger, this desire to constantly advance in my relationship with the Lord. I want more and more of Jesus every day and less and less of me. I want people to see Jesus in me. I want to go tell the world the good news of Jesus and to make disciples.

Because of Jesus, my wife got the husband she had always deserved, my kids got the father they needed, my parents got the son they knew I could be, and my church received a brother in Christ. If Jesus can do this for me, He can do it for anyone, including you. It all starts with surrendering to Him.

[Gold]
When I think of heaven, I think of being covered by the light and love of Jesus. Every earthly thought and question I might have will no longer matter. My body will be made new with no more sickness, sadness, or pain. I believe I will want to just sit quietly, facedown, and worship. I think the sights of heaven will be amazing. I'll get to see streets of gold, beautiful gates of precious gems, and a majestic sea. I will find and reunite with old family and friends. Heaven will be an eternity of perfect peace and rest.

[Final Thoughts]
A friend of mine posed a question to me that helps motivate me to serve God daily. He asked, "If you worked for a business and your only job was to make disciples, would your boss want two of you?" I want to be a man who follows Jesus with everything I've got and shares His love with everyone I meet!

words of [HOPE]

"I wait for the Lord,
my whole being waits,
and in his word I put my hope."
Psalm 130:5

If God is sovereign, and He is, then He is not shocked at our mistakes, our struggles, and the weights that crush us most. Could He just take them away? Of course! But our greatest moments of growth are not found on the mountaintops but in the depth of the valleys. It is there that we see our emptiness and find Christ's fulfillment. It is there that we look at our weakness and see Christ's strength. It is there that we realize our frailty and the eternality that Christ offers. All of our struggles — and no man is on "struggling island" alone — are indeed doing something. They are a blessing. They are an odd reason to rejoice. Though they certainly do not feel light or momentary, they are producing something!

"So we do not lose heart. Though our outer self is wasting away, our inner self is being renewed day by day. For this light momentary affliction is preparing us for an eternal weight of glory beyond all comparison, as we look not to the things that are seen but to the things that are unseen." (2 Corinthians 4:16-18)

Only a sovereign God could use our moments of greatest pain to produce a beautiful masterpiece . . . and He does.

Troy Nicholson

Larry Don's Story

[Gray]

I grew up in a home with a great mom and dad. We moved several times growing up, but I went to the same school which made me happy. I had good friends who I didn't want to leave. School, sports, and my two younger brothers kept my family busy always doing something.

I was taught who God was at an early age. Between the ages of six to about 12 years old we attended two different churches. God was never the most important thing in the life of our family. Like many families, we went to church when it was convenient. Although we weren't real devout, my mom always told us God was real, and it was very important to believe in Him.

Around the age of 12 we stopped going to church, but I had friends who went. I would go with them sometimes and I enjoyed it. Although I didn't know a whole lot about religion, I did have a basic understanding of many important things like the Bible, Jesus, heaven and hell. I was happy to still get to go to church camp in the summer at Siloam Springs, and that's where God became real to me.

[Red]

The worship nights were fun at camp. Much more interesting than the Sunday morning sermons. I realize now it's because they are specifically designed for that age group. During one of the nights of worship at camp I experienced Jesus. I felt like He wanted me to go forward and pray for forgiveness. At the time I wasn't sure why, but now I realize it was the Holy Spirit speaking to my spirit. God was drawing me to Himself.

There is something called the "Romans Road to Salvation" that many people have used to explain every person's need for God. It's a collection of verses out of the book of Romans which explains God's plan for salvation.

Romans 3:23 says "...for all have sinned and fall short of the glory of God..."

Romans 6:23 goes on to say, "For the wages of sin is death, but the free gift of God is eternal life in Christ Jesus our Lord."

Then in Romans 5:8 it says, "But God demonstrates His own love toward us, in that while we were yet sinners, Christ died for us." And since Christ died for us we can be saved.

Romans 10:9 tells us, "...that if you confess with your mouth Jesus is Lord, and believe in your heart that God raised Him from the dead, you will be saved."

God opened my eyes to see that I was a sinner in need of a Savior, and Jesus was offering me the gift of salvation.

[White]

I went forward to the altar. One of the children's leaders from our church prayed with me for salvation. I didn't understand everything there is to know about God, but I truly believed in Jesus as my Savior at the time. I was excited to embrace God, and I really felt like He had changed something inside of me.

[Blue]

After getting back from church camp, I was baptized. When I went to the back to get ready they gave me a choir robe to wear. At the time, I felt like it was something very special. I understood what salvation and baptism meant, but I didn't really understand what it meant to have a day-to-day relationship with God. The examples around me weren't the best. Soon my family moved and we quit going to church regularly. Not a good combination for a new teenage Christian.

[Green]

Fortunately, as I got older, I developed some friendships with people who had more of a church background than I did. They invited me to attend church services and events with them. I also got involved with the Fellowship of Christian Athletes through sports at my school. I wasn't in a healthy relationship with Jesus, but I truly believe God used these friends and FCA to be in my life to keep me from straying much further away from Him than I did.

Toward the end of high school, I got away from sports and my Christian friends. Naturally, without these relationships and the influence of church in my life, I drifted further and further away from Jesus. As I got older, into my early 20's, I wasn't living a Christian lifestyle at all. I got married, had three kids, and worked a lot. God wasn't ever discussed between me and my wife. I still believed in God but didn't have any idea of the importance He could make in my daily life. My wife had some bad experiences in church growing up, and she didn't like the idea of organized religion, which was fine with me.

My mom was always telling me that I needed to get back into church. She would say it was important for me and my family. I guess she realized the difference it made for her when she went compared to when she didn't. I didn't listen to her. I would tell her, "I know mom." It was my business, not hers. But God has a way of getting someone's attention! God would eventually use my mom to draw me and several other members of my family into a deep, fulfilling relationship with Him.

In 2003, my wife and I were going through some hard times. I had begun drinking alcohol regularly back in high school, and it had escalated as I got older. Eventually, I was a full blown alcoholic. I had a terrible mouth, and I was not a loving husband. My wife ended up leaving me. Shortly after she left, the company I worked for closed down, and I couldn't find another job. I was getting to the end of my rope.

On July 3rd, I went on an 18 hour drinking binge. I drank heavily from 9 a.m. until 3 a.m. the next morning. Early in the morning on July 4th, I had a near death experience sitting on the floor of an empty hotel bathroom. A terrible, dark, hideous fear of death overcame me. Terrified, I swore I would never touch alcohol again if I could live. I immediately gave up drinking and have been sober ever since that night. I cleaned up and apologized to my wife. She forgave me, and we reconciled our differences.

Although I believed God had saved my life and restored my marriage through that horrible experience, I wasn't ready to fully follow Him yet. By 2009, I was working for a great company. My wife and I had worked through our problems, and we were happy. Then I got a phone call that would change my life forever.

My mom called and told me she had been diagnosed with pancreatic cancer. They gave her six months to live. She made it to seven. After her passing, my 17 year-old son took it hard. This turned out to be what God used to get his attention and eventually mine.

When my son turned 19 he started going to church regularly and got real with God. He was baptized at 21 years old and started taking his little brother with him to church. When his little brother got baptized, my wife and I began going to church with them.

I realized the God who had saved me so many years ago at camp was still right there waiting for me to come back to Him. He had never left. Although I ignored our relationship, He never abandoned me. His long-suffering love is truly incredible.

My wife had always had issues with organized religion for as long as I had known her. After we agreed to attend church with our boys, her heart softened to the love of Jesus. Though her painful past from religious organizations was enormous, the love of God turned out to be greater. Amazingly, she got baptized and heavily involved in our church. She loves worshiping and serving in our church to this day.

Since then, God has become our first love, and our love for one another has grown deeper than we ever imagined it could have. We love going to church now! We have enjoyed Sundays, Wednesday nights, small group Bible studies, and discipleship classes. My oldest son has been ordained and recently baptized his older sister. My youngest son and I serve in our church worship band. He is our drummer, and I play the bass guitar.

God has put me in a position to speak at men's meetings and to the youth at our church. I have begun teaching the third through fifth graders on Wednesday nights. I'm not really comfortable speaking to groups, especially in church, but I shared my testimony in church recently. While it was uncomfortable, I know being obedient to God is helping me grow in my walk with Jesus.

I've connected with other men's ministries and have helped feed the homeless in our area. I had a very special experience with my oldest son when we visited a prison ministry. I was proud of him, watching the way he treated those men. He had no judgement or condemnation for them, but only showed the genuine love of Jesus to them.

My church is important to me, because it gives me people to do life with. We have developed great friendships with many people there. We love each other and help with spiritual and physical needs. I want to continue growing as a Christian man and leader.

[Gold]

I look forward to a glorious reunion in heaven with my Mom. I can't wait to tell her how right she was about Jesus. There are other family members I also want to see and many friends who have already gone before me. I believe heaven will be a place with no more fear and no more pain. How awesome will that be?

[Final Thoughts]

No matter what you have going on in your life or what you might be facing, you are never too far away from God to come back. Many times, I thought I was too far gone, but Jesus was right there the whole time. If He will do that for me, He will do that for you.

words of [WISDOM]

"If you accept the expectations of others, especially negative ones, then you never will change the outcome."
- Michael Jordan

Alcoholism results in drinking becoming everything in your life, even at the expense of your livelihood, your health, and your relationships. Attempts to stop drinking can result in tremors or hallucinations. Therapy, detox, and rehab can help you get your life back. [3]

"Wine is a mocker and beer a brawler; whoever is led astray by them is not wise."
- King David
Proverbs 20:1

Jimmy's Story

[Gray]

I was born the middle child of five kids in Fort Lee, Virginia to a black father and Australian mother. I only have a few memories of living with my biological parents, because they were divorced when I was six years old. My second oldest brother and I went to live with my dad, so I was separated from my mom and three of my siblings.

Eventually, after a couple of years, my aunt and uncle adopted me as their son. I began referring to them as mom and dad, because they were much more like parents to me than my biological parents ever were.

My new mother was an active member of the church, and I was immediately introduced to it. Sunday school, worship service, choir, Vacation Bible School, and the Baptist Training Union became what my life revolved around.

[Red]

I began hearing regularly about how Jesus loves me. I even knew it in my head, but I didn't completely believe it in my heart. I had been hurt by my parents abandoning me, so understanding my heavenly Father's unconditional love was tough.

When I was 10 years old, my brother and I were sitting in a church service together, and I remember feeling like I needed to go forward and ask Jesus to forgive me of my sins. When the time came at the end of the service, I asked my brother to go up to the front with me. He agreed to go with me to the altar. The pastor came over to where we were and prayed with us. I confessed with my mouth "Jesus is Lord" and believed in my heart God raised him from the dead, and I was saved. My brother also got saved. It meant a lot to me for us to get saved at the same time.

I remember how special the moment was when I received God's gift of salvation. I felt different. I knew something had changed inside of me.

[Blue]

I told my mom what had happened, and she was happy for us. The next week we were scheduled to get baptized. I remember her getting me a white robe to wear for the ceremony. The baptistry in our church had a picture of Jesus being baptized by John the Baptist on the wall behind it. I thought it was a beautiful painting. I remember walking out into the water, in front of everyone, and publicly identifying myself as a follower of Jesus. Then my pastor submerged me under the water, and I felt like this was something very special. Although I've made many mistakes since then, I know I believed in Jesus then and have never felt like I should be baptized again.

[Green]

Along with my church activities, I played a lot of sports. During the summer I played baseball and softball. Once fall rolled around you could find me on the basketball court. My father owned a dry cleaning business where I learned to press clothes. This allowed me to avoid farm work in a community where the major income was from farming. My dad also owned rent houses and a boarding house. Needless to say, I was raised in a well-to-do family. We were much better off than most of the black people in the area.

This, along with the fact that I looked different than most kids because of my mixed ethnicity, led to me being picked on a lot. I was mistaken for being Mexican or Latino much of the time. Being mixed race wasn't easy. I was teased and called a half breed regularly. This hurt my feelings and left deep emotional scars.

My parents also owned a fast food business called The Custard Stand. It was located in the middle of all the businesses known as Jig Joints. These were pool halls and bars where food and beer was served. There were also some nightclubs in the area.

As I got older and began hanging out at these businesses, my viewpoint changed from being influenced primarily by religious thoughts and ideas to a radically different worldly point of view. Deep down, I was always trying to fill that empty place of being displaced from my biological family. So I found many "brothers and sisters" to party with instead. I found out later most of them only hung out with me because I was willing to spend my money on them.

My new "mother" never wanted to discuss my past, insisting she was my mom now. She was very loving to me, and I always loved her dearly. But there were things about my past, rumors I picked up on, and things told to me that I wanted to know the truth about. This led to me developing an inferiority complex and being easily offended. I compensated for my low self-esteem by manipulating people, especially women, to get what I wanted.

By the time I was in high school I was sexually active. I also began to experiment with alcohol. Sex and alcohol became the way I hid from my low self-esteem. I found after a few drinks I felt much better about myself, and that liquid courage helped me be even more confident with the girls. My identity in high school became playing sports and partying.

After I graduated I went to college. During my college years, I started using marijuana on a daily basis. I would still attend a church service occasionally, and deep-down inside of me, I knew I wasn't living right.

I got married and we were together for 12 years until she passed away. This left me with three children to raise. My parents helped out a lot during this time of my life.

I turned to drugs and alcohol to relieve my pain and frustration. I began to drink heavily, and my drug use increased and expanded to using cocaine. I entered a treatment center for the first time to try to gain some control back over my life. After being released, I remarried to my current wife, and we moved to Little Rock, Arkansas. I got a job with the postal service.

For the next ten years I tried everything I could to convince myself I could beat my substance abuse issues. I would manage to stay sober for short periods of time. After several visits to inpatient and outpatient treatment centers, I had become a professional patient. I knew exactly what to expect when I walked through those doors. I lost all hope and didn't even like myself anymore.

When I would lay off drugs and alcohol for a few days, my mind would clear up and I would think about God. I believed in Him and knew He had done some things in my life, like keeping me safe from almost being shot and saving me from a few episodes of overdosing.

I wanted God to be in my life again. I just didn't believe I was good enough for Him. I didn't like feeling weak or humbling myself. It was frustrating, because I knew I had major problems emotionally and financially with my employment and my marriage. Instead of dealing with one issue at a time, I would try to tackle them all together and end up being overwhelmed. Then I would run back to drugs and alcohol to forget my problems.

In the winter of 2000, I was in one of my worst states of mind. I was in the familiar cycle of losing my job, being behind on my bills, and my family not wanting to be around me. I hadn't been to church in a few years and didn't want to hear about God's love, but I knew deep down I needed something.

In January of 2001, I went to a treatment center. I was beaten down and emotionally unstable. This time was different. I kept my mouth shut and listened to the people there about how to remain sober. Although I had listened to these words before, I really heard them this time.

After getting the drugs and alcohol out of my system, I agreed to join an outpatient recovery program, as well as Alcoholics Anonymous and Cocaine Anonymous programs. Here I developed a new set of friends to help me fight my demons. My sponsor helped me work through the 12-step program and I began to live one day at a time. This time, when I felt tempted to go back to alcohol or drugs, I had a support system to help me win the battle.

God was discussed in all of our meetings, but remaining sober was really my overriding focus. Over the next few years, I learned to enjoy helping others find the freedom I had found from substance abuse.

I began going to church regularly and reading my Bible over this time. God began to work in my heart. Although I still didn't feel good enough to be considered a child of God, the truth of the Bible opened my eyes. No, I wasn't good enough, but Jesus still loved me. He doesn't judge me on my merit, but on His sacrifice on the cross. He won the battle, so I could be saved.

What I thought I had lost began to reappear in my life. My faith level increased, and I was healing. What I had been chasing my whole life, I now had received: peace of mind.

"One day at a time", "This too shall pass", and "Let go and let God" became phrases I proclaimed regularly to help me win daily battles. Although I know I'm saved and forgiven, I never want to forget how bad my life was during my addiction. It hurt me and everyone I loved deeply. Remembering how dark life is without Jesus helps me stay on the straight and narrow path.

I'm now 17 years sober. I never want to go back to using drugs. I warn doctors not to prescribe me narcotics. Life today is so much better than before. My marriage has healed, and God is healing hurts with other members of my family. The best thing I can do today is continue to follow Jesus and stay sober.

I'm retired now but still active. My church is my support system now. Our pastor, Larry Charles, is a godly man who inspires me to follow Jesus. My church has loved and supported me through the loss of several family members, and they love me unconditionally.

I'm not perfect, but I try not to get overwhelmed when I make a mistake. As long as I stay sober throughout a day, I consider it a good day. I know with God's help I can keep winning my battles.

I'm thankful for my parents who raised me in a loving home, for my wife who loved me even in the darkest times, and for all those who prayed for me when I was hopeless. When I started this journey of sobriety, all I wanted was to not use drugs or alcohol. God has given me so much more. I have a purpose for living each day, and that is loving and helping others. I have a family who I love. I have friends in my wonderful church who I can do life with. And I can wake up each day knowing God is with me and I am His!

[Gold]

Heaven, to me, is a place where God will sit on His Throne and watch over His people. I will be in my glorified body and able to see God. No more sickness and death, no more worries, no more pain. I hope to see my mother and father and all my family members. And when I enter my dwelling place, it will be more beautiful than anything I can imagine. The most exciting thing about going to Heaven is there will be everlasting peace.

[Final Thoughts]

I hate that my kids had to witness my life during my addiction, but I'm happy my grandkids don't. That is a blessing. I fight my battle one day at a time, and I never take a day I remain sober for granted. I like to say, "It works if you work it; won't if you don't." If God can do this for me, He can most assuredly do it for you! But you will have to fight for it. So get to fighting!

words of [HOPE]

There are a number of things we lose in this life — hair, weight, a loved one, a job or even a home — but one thing we can't afford to lose is hope. Hope is the umbrella that keeps us dry during the torrential downpours of life. Hope is that which keeps us afloat in the floods of life. Hope is that which gives us the strength to take another step when we can't see where our foot will fall. This hope that I speak of is not what the world calls a wish. No; this hope that the believer has is based on an assurance in the faithfulness of God! This hope is a confidence that what God said is true. This is a hope like that which Abraham had when, "He staggered not at the promise of God through unbelief, but was strong in faith giving glory to God and being fully persuaded that what he had promised, he was also able to perform."
Romans 4:20-21

Let me show you **H.O.P.E.**

H - Help for the helpless. "God is our refuge and strength, an ever-present help in trouble." (Psalm 46:1)

O - Omnipotent (having unlimited power; able to do anything). Your confidence is not in some weak, milquetoast (timid or feeble) individual, but in our all-powerful God! "Now to him who is able to do immeasurably more than all we ask or imagine, according to his power that is at work within us..." (Ephesians 3:20)

P - Provider. Where God guides, He will provide. That may sound cliché, but it's still the truth. "And my God will meet all your needs according to the riches of his glory in Christ Jesus." (Philippians 4:19)

E - Enough. Hope is coming to the realization that God is enough. His grace is sufficient for us. Hang in there. There is hope. "Three times I pleaded with the Lord to take it away from me. But he said to me, "My grace is sufficient for you, for my power is made perfect in weakness." Therefore I will boast all the more gladly about my weaknesses, so that Christ's power may rest on me." (2 Corinthians 12:8-9)

Pastor Larry L. Charles

Gin's Story

[Gray]

My mother was single and living at home with her alcoholic parents when I was prematurely born. She told me that I was so small they could fit me into a women's size five shoe box.

When I was one, my mother married her first husband who was an alcoholic and hard core drug addict. He was extremely abusive to my mother, myself, and my four little brothers. When I was only 18 months old, he intentionally poured Tabasco sauce in my face, causing me to get cataracts in both eyes. Eventually, my mother started using meth with him.

I knew more about drugs than any child should ever know. Instead of having a normal childhood, I had to be the responsible grown up. Taking on the responsibilities of my parents, I did the laundry, grocery shopping, cooking, and cleaned the house...when we had one. One Christmas, I had my grandma take the money out of my savings account she had for me, so I could buy presents for my little brothers. Mom had spent all of our money on drugs.

At the age of 10, my mother's first husband set our hallway on fire, then made me and my brothers' walk through it. Later that same night, he set his brother's house on fire with 15 people inside of it. My mother, my brothers, and I were six of the 15 people inside. He was later sentenced to a minimum security prison in California for two counts of arson and 15 counts of attempted murder.

During his prison sentence my mom started dating one of her dealers. At the age of 11, I remember finding an 8-ball of meth on the back of our toilet. I called my brother into the bathroom and explained to him what it was. I convinced him to flush it, because I didn't want to touch it. Unfortunately, this wasn't unusual for us.

My mom and her boyfriend decided to get clean and then get married. Just after I turned 12, my new stepdad decided I needed to meet my real dad. In the summer of 1990, I flew to Arkansas to meet my daddy. On my first night in Arkansas, I met the person who would later help save my life and find a relationship with God. His name was Greg Jenson. He was best friends with my brother James. I wasn't aware of it at the time, but Greg said he fell in love with me the first time he laid eyes on me.

41

When I was 13 my mom and stepdad moved us to Tonasket, Washington. A little while later, when I turned 14, my mom sent me to live with my dad in Arkansas. I started dating Greg right away. On November 14th, 1992 my dad left early in the morning to go deer hunting. He never returned. He died that day in a hunting accident. My father's death sent me into a deep depression.

My mom made me move back to Washington. I was filled with anger — angry at the world, angry I didn't get to know my dad longer, angry I had to leave Greg, angry with my mother because after she got sober she was diagnosed with multiple personality disorder. I felt like my only chance at a normal life had been ripped away from me. I started smoking pot and drinking. Nobody cared anyway.

When I was 16, I started dating my best friend in Washington and soon got pregnant. When I was five months pregnant he asked me to marry him and I said yes. I didn't love him, but he was my way out. After my daughter was born, I started smoking crack with him. We got married. It was one wrong decision after another. Our entire marriage was about the drugs we were doing. I went on a drug run with my then mother-in-law and we were raped by the drug dealers. We told my husband and father-in-law what had happened. They went out to the cabins to confront them. When they returned, I was handed three grams of drugs and told never to speak of it again.

Our marriage didn't last very long after that. I knew I was in no shape to be raising my daughter, so I gave my parents custody of her. At the age of 24, I moved to Idaho, where I became a bartender at a little hole-in-the-wall bar. It didn't take me long to find the wrong crowd. I started dating a meth cooker and using it regularly. Because of who I was running with, I was soon being watched by the police. One night, I was at the bar when the head of the drug task force came in and took me in for questioning. Idaho is a "No Tolerance" state, which means they don't have to have proof, only hearsay, to arrest you. They eventually charged me with aiding and abetting the distribution of methamphetamine. This held a prison sentence of 25 years to life. I was facing more prison time than if I had been the actual manufacturer of the drugs.

After spending a few weeks in jail, I was bailed out. While I was out on bail waiting for my trial, I was walking down the street at night with snow up to my hips. I stopped in the middle of the street, and for the first time in my life, I prayed to God. I asked Him to give me a reason to straighten up, because I didn't have any hope.

Three days later, I found out I was pregnant. At that moment, I went clean. I immediately poured the dope I had in my pockets out and cleaned out all the rest. I was soon offered a plea bargain. If I pleaded guilty they would give me a class C felony. I took the plea deal and moved back to Washington. A little while later, I had my beautiful baby boy.

When my son was 17 months old, I met a man who I thought was perfect. He wasn't like anyone I'd ever dated, or so I thought. He was an ex-marine and treated me so well. One night when we first started dating we stayed up all night talking about all our hopes, dreams, and fears. I told him my biggest fear was to end up with someone who would abuse one of my children. Over the next few years he brought my biggest fears to life. He broke me like I'd never been broken before. He alienated me from all my family and friends, making me totally dependent on him. I wasn't allowed to work or have a life of my own for that matter.

Eventually, three Pierce County deputies were at my front door to arrest him for sexual assault on a minor. The minor was my oldest son. I felt like I could die. Two days later child protective services took my youngest two boys away from me for failing to protect their older brother. After being clean for seven years, I called a friend and told him to come smoke some meth with me. I couldn't handle my reality without it.

After some other horrific experiences, my life kept spiraling out of control. I was homeless and strung out on the streets of Tacoma. I can remember sitting on the steps of a laundry mat yelling at God, crying and asking Him why he didn't let me die. Why was I left to live this horrible life? I felt completely dead on the inside. I didn't feel loved in any way, shape, or form.

[Red]

I began talking to Greg Jensen on Facebook. I told him how awful my life was, and he said he was buying me a bus ticket to come visit him and my brothers in Arkansas. The only catch was I couldn't use drugs during my trip. I agreed to his conditions.

After a wonderful visit I decided this is where I needed to be. I got a job and a place of my own. I flew out to get my youngest two boys. My oldest son stayed with my mom. The first Sunday after I got them to

43

Arkansas my cousin called inviting me to her church. I agreed to go only to appease her. The moment I stepped inside of Grace Church something awakened in me.

[White]

I accepted another invitation to attend a special night Grace Church was having. Jesus reached out to me that evening. I remember sitting there listening to the lady on the stage talk about how Jesus doesn't care if we are rich or poor. He doesn't care if we keep our house spotless, but what he does care about is if we accept him into our hearts and our lives. God's love overwhelmed me, and I started crying. They asked if anyone was ready to accept Jesus into their heart. I went to the altar with my cousin and moved from death to life.

[Blue]

On October 22nd, 2017, just a little over two years of being sober, I was baptized at Grace Church. I cried tears of joy and felt more at peace than I ever had in my whole life. I felt like I was finally safe and loved.

[Green]

The stronger my faith gets, the easier it is to deal with the struggles which come my way. I still struggle, but my struggles don't define who I am. Jesus defines who I am. I can now walk around with my head held high. I know that no matter what I face, Jesus is with me every step of the way. I have real relationships with real people. I have given my life to the Lord, and in return He has made me whole again. He has restored my life.

My oldest son is doing well and still lives with my mom in Washington. I love when he gets to visit. I have gained custody of my youngest two sons. I'm also in the process of legally adopting my youngest daughter, Sariah. She was a little miracle who I took in from a girl who was pregnant and going to give her up. God used Sariah to inspire me to dig deep into the Bible and my faith.

I have recently realized that God didn't let me die, because He had a plan for me. He always knew I'd be where I am right now, joyfully raising my youngest three children in a good Christian home.

[Gold]

I believe heaven is going to be like earth, only better. There won't be any chaos, suffering, or pain. It will be like the Garden of Eden was before sin, when it was perfect, peaceful, and beautiful. There won't be anything negative or bad. Heaven will be beautiful and full of happiness forever.

[Final Thoughts]

God doesn't call the equipped, He equips the called. Jesus has blessed me more than I ever thought He could. I'm a loving, mistake making, and worthwhile child of God.

words of [WISDOM]

"I avoid looking forward or backward, and try to
keep looking upward."
- Charlotte Brontë

---

*"One thing I do: forgetting what lies behind and reaching forward to
what lies ahead, I press on toward the goal for the prize of the upward call
of God in Christ Jesus."*
- Paul the Apostle
Philippians 3:13b-14

"It always seems impossible until it's done."
- Nelson Mandela

Johnny's Story

[Gray]

My story started in 1945, when I was born to a 16 year-old single mother. Two years later, she fell in love with and married my Dad, the father who raised me as his own. They provided me and my three brothers a good home and taught us morals and manners.

Growing up, my family went to church regularly, so I knew about Jesus, but I didn't really *know* Him. All I really understood was the Bible had a lot of exciting stories in it. When I was 12 or 13 years old, after a week of attending Vacation Bible School, an invitation was given to come forward if you wanted to be saved. I still didn't understand exactly what that meant. But all my friends went forward, and not wanting to be left out, I went too. We were given a three by five card to write our names on and told to bring our parents the following day so that we could be baptized. So I did, and the next day I was baptized in Horseshoe Lake.

I didn't really understand much of what I was doing, and the church was a small country church who couldn't afford a full time preacher. No one there ever asked if I was a sinner or even if I knew what sin was. There wasn't anyone there to disciple me or teach me how to have a relationship with Christ.

I graduated from high school when I was 17 years old. Not wanting to go to college or be a farmer, I joined the Army. It was my first time away from home on my own. I trained to be a medic in an Air Ambulance Unit in Vietnam where I was introduced to morphine.

When I returned home, I brought a habit home that I couldn't control. It was very difficult for me to get morphine in the states. So, being stationed at Fort Sam Houston, Texas, I started making trips to Mexico where I could get heroin.

During this time, my relationship with God and His church was non-existent. It was all about me, and no one else mattered. I continued to make one bad decision after another. I went AWOL from the Army and started committing armed robbery to support my heroin habit.

About a year later, I was arrested for armed robbery in Memphis, Tennessee. I received a dishonorable discharge from the Army, and I was sentenced to 10 years hard labor. Time in prison wasn't about

47

rehabilitation, it was about punishment. After serving five years, five months, and five days, I was released on parole.

I hadn't learned anything except how to be more careful in my criminal enterprises. I didn't learn the lesson well enough, because five years and two failed marriages later, I was arrested for receiving stolen property. This one cost me a year and one day in prison.

My bad decisions continued for another 20 years, staying just one step ahead of the law. I was terrible at relationships, adding two more failed marriages and two children to my list of failures. I used people and then moved on, always thinking that a change of location or a change of partners would bring me happiness. During this time, I got into manufacturing and dealing meth.

I moved back to Arkansas with wife number five. I found out later that we had left just hours before I was to be arrested for drug manufacturing and sales in California. I had risen to the Most Wanted Man status in California. We bought 40 acres just outside of Hardy, Arkansas. After a year and a half, my wife decided she was tired of life with me and moved back to California.

The manufacturing of drugs and partying continued. After all, now I wasn't accountable to anyone. After a while, I realized I didn't have one true friend. They all wanted something from me and were offering nothing in return. I had lots of stuff — land, a house, boat, camper, motorcycle, truck, and car — but I wasn't happy or even content. I was lonely, even around all those people, and I felt empty inside.

[Red]

On my 54th birthday, after partying and doing meth for about a week with several friends, I realized there wasn't a single person I cared for or trusted. Deep depression and anger set in. The next morning, just before daylight, I became irate and began yelling for everyone to leave. Some ignored me until I grabbed my pistol!

After everyone was gone, I made a cup of coffee and sat down on my porch. I planned to watch the sun rise and then kill myself. But as I was sitting there watching the sunshine through the leaves and the deer grazing in my yard, I started talking to God.

I told Him, if He was real, to give me some sort of sign. I couldn't go on living like I had been anymore, empty and alone, separated from everyone and everything. As I watched the deer grazing closer and closer to where I was sitting, the sun's rays beamed through the leaves, and my dogs who would normally bark and chase the deer, were ignoring them. As the deer came within a few yards from where I was sitting, I realized I had my sign. God revealed Himself to me in the peace of that moment.

[White]

I submitted my life entirely to Jesus. I told Him if He would help me, I would go anywhere and do anything He wanted. I confessed I was a sinner and begged for His forgiveness. I asked Him to be my Lord and Savior! He said, "Let Go", and I did. Peace flooded my soul. I knew He was real and loved me. I believed Romans 10:9, "If you confess with your mouth, 'Jesus is Lord,' and believe in your heart that God raised him from the dead, you will be saved."

I flushed all of my drugs, poured out all of my alcohol, and started putting out the word that no more drugs would be used at my house. God began changing me that day. I didn't know how to be a Christian or read my Bible. I clung to a verse I ran across, Philippians 2:13 "For it is God who is at work in you, both to will and to work for *His* good pleasure."

I allowed a guy I knew to move into a camper I had on my property with the understanding there would be no drugs or drug use there. Unfortunately for me, he was stealing pills to make meth and storing them in my camper. He got busted, and to get reduced charges, he turned me in as a meth cook.

When the police showed up, I wasn't worried, because I had been clean for almost a year. When they found his pills in the camper, I explained to them they weren't mine. I was still arrested. Their reasoning was: my property, my stuff. So I was taken to the Fulton County jail and charged with the manufacture, possession, and sale of meth. I had no way to make my $100,000 bail to get out of jail.

I couldn't understand why God would let this happen to me! At first, I was mad and angry with God. Then I remembered telling Him, "I will go anywhere and do anything you want". After that, I was at peace with anything God had in store for me.

Miraculously God orchestrated my release from jail after six weeks, although my charges were still pending. I was allowed to move to another county to live with my parents and find a job.

Three months later, I went to my 40 year class reunion where I ran into a beautiful Christian lady I had known since the fourth grade. We didn't talk much, but the following Monday she called to ask if I would like to go to church with her. That was our first date. We fell in love and 62 days later we were married.

She married me knowing I was going to prison and not knowing for how long. One month later, I asked my lawyer to make the best deal he could. I agreed to plead guilty, so I could get on with my life. The best deal he could get me was 10 years, because of all my prior convictions.

I was sent to the Varner Unit, maximum security. Praise God there was a new program starting in the prisons called the PAL program. It allowed inmates who were in the program to live together and be instructed on how to apply God's Word to our everyday lives. I was in a program where God was filling me up with His word, and I was learning how to have an authentic relationship with Him.

After finishing that program, I volunteered to participate in the substance abuse treatment program offered there. This class helped me understand some of the things that caused me to make some of the choices I had made. God allowed me to be released from my 10 year prison sentence after 20 months. I returned to my wife, my job, and my church family.

[Blue]

I attended a revival service where the preacher taught about baptism. He pointed out in the Bible where there is an order to our obedience to God. We are told to be saved and then to be baptized. Although I had been baptized as a child, I knew I hadn't been saved until much later. I wanted to get things in the correct biblical order.

I was baptized a short time later. It is important to me to be as obedient as I can to what the Bible teaches. It was a special experience to publicly follow through in believers' baptism as a true believer.

[Green]

A friend of mine kept inviting me to come to a Celebrate Recovery meeting with him. I couldn't understand why, because by that time I had been clean for over nine years. Surely I didn't need another program. I finally agreed to go just so he would get off my back.

I thought Celebrate Recovery was only for people with drug or alcohol problems, but I quickly realized that it covered many other issues as well. Shortly after I started going, the guy running the program quit. The church leaders asked if I would be willing to take over. I told them I wasn't qualified, but I would pray about it.

After much prayer and research, I agreed to lead it if they would send me to the summit meeting in California. I learned a lot and met some amazing people. I started enlisting people to help me get the program up and started. Sixteen of us went through the step studies and advanced leadership training. After 18 months of prayer and preparation, we had our first large group meeting. It went great!

As I worked through the steps, I learned a lot about myself and my relationship with God. Celebrate Recovery helps me face the problems that continue to arise in my life with honest, biblical principles. I have watched God use this program to change hundreds of lives, including mine.

[Gold]

There are many things about heaven that excite me! Worshipping and praising Jesus face to face will be amazing. Exploring and enjoying a never ending perfect place will be incredible. It's thrilling to think about my true home that Jesus is building for me.

[Final Thoughts]

My favorite verse is Proverbs 3:6, "In all your ways acknowledge Him, and He will make your paths straight." Thanks only to Jesus Christ, I stand before you today as a forgiven drug addict, alcoholic, thief, cheat, and adulterer, who by God's grace and faith in Christ Jesus, has been clean and sober for over 20 years. And, He will do the same for you if you will follow Him!

words of [HOPE]

"Let us hold unswervingly to the hope we profess,
for he who promised is faithful."
Hebrews 10:23

Bound up. Tied up. In over our head. Stuck. Drowning. Dying. In the death grip of addiction. In the chains of sin. All of us have been there.

Oh the hope of the GOSPEL. Jesus comes to live among us. He is tempted just like we are. He has to resist taking that first deadly step toward addiction. He walks through this life without sin. He knows all my junk and messed up stuff. He knows all your junk and messed up stuff. Still, Jesus marches to the cross. Still, He lays down His life for me, for you — dying a death we all deserve. Dying in our place. For our addiction. For our sin. Then He conquers it all by coming back from the dead. He conquers our sin. He conquers our addiction. He frees us.

This is the reason all of these stories you are reading here exist. This is the reason we can all experience freedom.

Kyle Lewallen

Tonya's Story

[Gray]

Life wasn't easy for me growing up. Being one of six kids raised by a mom on welfare was tough. When I was only a year old my parents divorced, but not before my dad left his pattern of abuse, addiction, and destruction upon us all.

I was a very shy, fearful girl in a loud house. My three older siblings, two sisters, and brother were always fighting and in conflict. Countless times the three youngest kids were spectators to the older kids fighting, cursing, and acting crazy. Mom had no help and no control over these situations. The louder the house got the quieter and more fearful I became.

Food became my only source of comfort in a home where the only emotion shown was anger. The words "I love you" seemed so foreign to me, but it's what I desired to hear so much. This chaotic early life situation set the stage for me experiencing many years of negative feelings and low self-esteem.

Occasionally, my mom would take us to church but never regularly. On the other hand, my mom's brother was diligent to take us to Vacation Bible School and children's church. He was one of the bright spots in an otherwise unhappy childhood. He made a positive impact in my life.

My brother was always drunk or high which made my home dysfunctional during my teenage years. Some family friends offered for me to move in with them, so at the age of sixteen I did. This was the first time in my life where I experienced a home where there was peace.

When I was 17 years old I met my first boyfriend who, two years later, became my first husband. He was my everything, and I loved him in spite of his lack of respect for me. I thought my love could change him into a better man. I had my first son at age 21 and my second one at age 23. I was the best mom I knew how to be, yet the cycle of verbal abuse and anger flowed over into my kids' lives. They were robbed of the happy and healthy home they deserved.

After eight years of being a faithful wife, I found out my husband was cheating on me with one of my coworkers. I was devastated to say the least. I hurt for not only myself but for my sons. We had to start over building a new life.

After having my heart broken, I was determined to not get too close to anyone. I began making bad decisions on who I dated and spent time with. My second husband came along during this time. He was the man who introduced me to meth. During our chaotic six years of marriage I got a felony conviction for drugs and lost custody of my kids. This led to my second divorce.

I started seeing another man, Sam, and we were both meth addicts. Life got crazy as we increased our drug use and sexual immorality. After some crazy episodes with drugs, I decided to try and get clean. I entered a 28 day rehab facility. I stayed clean for 59 days, but the man I loved was always getting high. It didn't take long for me to cave and go back to using drugs.

I was in a huge trap and had no way out. My boyfriend, Sam, ended up going to prison. I was alone, strung out, and broke. I did still have a car, but I couldn't even afford to put gas in it. I was miserable and running wild without anything to live for.

Sam surrendered his heart and life to Jesus while in jail. He would write me letters telling me how he was praying for me, but I was still a wreck and didn't know where to go for help. I was just living day-to-miserable-day like I had been doing the previous 10 years. I was at the bottom of the bottom and had become everything I hated growing up. It would take me hours to write Sam a letter — when I would stop running long enough to write him. I hated myself and what I had allowed my life to become.

[Red]

I was so beat down that I wanted to die rather than live like this any longer. So, I prayed to a God I wasn't sure even existed. I asked, "God, if you are real, please send Sam home, so he can help me. I'd rather die than live like this another minute."

The very next day the guard told Sam to call home for a ride, because he was being released. I got the call and couldn't believe it. God answered my prayer. Could God be real? Could He love me after everything I had done? Could there be hope for my life? Still too scared to really believe in God, I told myself I would only believe it when I actually saw Sam come home.

[White]

The next day, when Sam stepped off that bus, God delivered me right then and there. In that moment, for the first time in 10 years, I could see clearly. God revealed his precious grace to me and shined his light on my life. Conviction for my many sins fell on me. I asked for forgiveness from God and from Sam. I didn't understand completely or even know how I knew, but without a doubt I was sure that ugly part of my life was over. I felt freedom for the first time in my life.

[Blue]

We connected with a great church led by Brother Kevin Edgar. I met with him to discuss being baptized. He did a wonderful job of making sure I understood what salvation meant and what my baptism signified.

Leading up to my baptism was an exciting time. I was so in love with Jesus. I wanted to do everything I could do to be as close to Him as possible. An overwhelming desire to be obedient to the command of Jesus to be baptized filled me.

Sam, my kids, and my church family were all there at our new church home on that Sunday morning. It felt like the awful, nasty, gross sin I had lived with for so long was washed away as I was submerged and came back up out of the water.

The day I got baptized everything felt new and clean. My mom made me a special dinner and food had never tasted so good. The peace and freedom I felt compared to the misery I had been trapped in is hard to put into words.

[Green]

Sam and I got into a good church and recovery program. We were married a few months after my baptism. We learned to love God most and He helps us to love others. The Lord is so good. It's only by His grace I am alive and free today. God has blessed me for the past 12 years with a beautiful marriage filled with love, respect and happiness.

God placed me in a good job. My husband became a jail minister. He's served in that capacity for over 12 years now, and we were recently able to purchase our first home. God has restored all we lost and blessed us with more than we could ever imagine. We are faithful members of a loving church, and I have a ministry where I write cards to people. I get to use my God-given gifts of helping and encouraging others through this endeavor.

I am a godly wife, mother, nana, daughter, sister, and friend today all because of God's grace. This is all through the love of Jesus. All glory, honor, and praise goes to my Almighty God!

In my family, He has rescued our daughter and her husband. They are serving Him in great ways, and the Lord is working on our sons and their families. We keep praying, leading by example and believing God will call them into His service. Thank you for this wonderful opportunity to share all God has done for me and where he has brought me from. If He can do this for me, He can do this for you!

[Gold]

I think heaven will be like a huge family reunion where I know everyone. I believe the beauty there will be more than I can wrap my mind around. I'm excited to go from soul to soul speaking to all the saints who went before me. I can imagine a long, long line of people waiting to see Jesus and to speak to our Father on the throne. I'm excited to see my brother, nephew, and so many other loved ones who have gone to heaven ahead of me.

[Final Thoughts]

Never stop believing the Lord is concerned about you or your family's salvation. If your kids or loved ones are caught up in addiction or aren't living in Christ, keep praying for the salvation of your family. No matter how bleak things may look, keep praying and being obedient to the Lord.

words of [WISDOM]

"Drugs and love don't mix. You either drop the drugs for what you love, or drop what you love for the drugs. There is no in between."
- Author Unknown

"For the grace of God has appeared that offers salvation to all people. It teaches us to say "No" to ungodliness and worldly passions, and to live self-controlled, upright and godly lives in this present age."
- Paul the Apostle
Titus 2:12

"You must do the things
you think you cannot do."
- Eleanor Roosevelt

Trey's Story

[Gray]

I never dreamed of becoming an addict as a kid. No one thinks, "I want to become a homeless junkie when I grow up." But that is where addiction led me. I grew up the only child of loving parents who did everything they could to make me happy. And I was happy! As a teenager, I spent lots of time hunting and fishing outside of school. My dream was to become a tournament fisherman. By my senior year in high school, I helped run the largest locally owned fishing tournament circuit in the state of Arkansas. It was a privilege to be able to fish and get to know some of the biggest names in the industry.

Once I graduated high school, I had a lot more free time. I began to spend that time with friends who were into partying. Drinking alcohol seemed like the normal thing to do as a teenager. I can remember the first time I ever got drunk like it was yesterday. I loved it! I loved how it made me feel and I didn't want to stop.

Once I started drinking, I didn't have the ability to stop. I would drink until I passed out. Eventually I came to a point where alcohol wasn't enough, so I moved on to other drugs. I started out with marijuana and I soon added pills. I mainly took hydros and Xanax, and I mixed them all up with alcohol, compounding the effect.

By this time, I was in my early 20's. Our parties moved to the nightclubs which led to more drinking and club drugs: ecstasy, cocaine, and amphetamines. Ecstasy and any type of upper or sexual drug became my new go to. Just like with alcohol and pills, my use of these drugs had no shut off button. Those who were around me would question me, "Man, are you sure you should keep going?" or "Don't you think you should sleep this off?"

I never wanted to stop. I was always the last to pass out, sometimes staying up for days. I did all of this while leading a "normal" life. I worked a 50 to 60 hour a week job and held down a house and all that comes with it. I was a "functioning addict" for almost 15 years.

At the age of 29 I became addicted to "bath salts", losing 100 pounds in just six months. It was during my early 30's when everything really started to fall apart in my life. The use of methamphetamines took over my life. I allowed that drug to take everything from me. I lost my wife, my house, and everything I owned. Drugs had taken everything but my life, and at the age of 34, I didn't want my life anymore either.

[Red]

I was raised in church, but I can't really say where my faith was as a kid. I didn't really have a faith of my own. As I got older, I became an atheist. I would have argued with a brick wall on how God wasn't real. And how dare anyone try and tell me that Jesus loved me? But on a November night in 2018, I cried out to God and He answered.

I thought I had hit the bottom about four or five times before, but I actually hit rock bottom on that night. In a rare moment of clarity, I realized how dark my life had become. On that November night, I had finally had enough.

I left where I was at, out in the middle of nowhere, with just my dog. I had no car, so we began walking. It was about a five mile walk to town. I remember about halfway through this walk, I just stopped and said something like, "God, if you are real, help me! I am scared, I am lost and I am tired."

I made it to a phone and decided to try to call my dad. He had stopped answering my calls for a long time, because my life was impacting him and my whole family very badly. I was surprised my dad actually answered the phone when I called! It was even more shocking when he agreed to pick me up, still not realizing what was going on. Now I understand what happened: God heard my heart cry, and the Holy Spirit was already at work, working through my dad.

He picked me up and drove me around for a little while, letting me use his phone. I was trying to get in touch with people who I thought were my friends. Thankfully no one answered.

[White]

That's when I honestly decided to surrender. I came to the end of myself and acknowledged Jesus as my Lord. I told my dad I wanted to change. He drove me to my grandmas and we started working on a plan. My family — the people I had stolen from, lied to, and repeatedly hurt — were the only ones there for me. They got me into a faith-based rehabilitation program.

I spent 30 days as an inpatient and another nine months in a chemical free house. I knew the 30 days wouldn't have been enough for me. Here is where I engulfed myself in the presence of the Holy Spirit, along with learning more about fighting addiction for nine months. When I wasn't at work or in groups, I spent my time alone with the Holy Spirit in my room, getting to know Him and having an intimate relationship with Jesus.

God spoke to me through the Apostle Paul's letters in the New Testament. One of the main things he talks about is the total renewal of the mind through Jesus Christ. It is possible. I am living proof. Going from the life I lived for so long, having so much hatred built up inside of me, to who I am now shows the power of the gospel. It's not just me either. This same gospel has been changing lives from the Apostle Paul to countless others throughout history.

[Blue]

As a teenager, I was baptized not understanding really anything about it, just doing what I thought I was supposed to do. This time was different. About seven or eight months after my true salvation, I was at church in our first service when my pastor, Perry Black, announced they were having a water baptism in the second service.

An overwhelming desire came over me to be baptized again. By this time, I was becoming sensitive to the Holy Spirit. I immediately went to speak with the proper leaders who discussed my desire and understanding. After our talk they agreed to allow me to be baptized immediately in the clothes I was wearing. My dad and step-mom were my only family members there. It meant a lot to me, because I know I was following what Jesus wanted me to do.

[Green]

Through God's power, I went from being a drug addicted atheist to a Holy Spirit filled man of God. I had an incredible experience where God poured out his spirit upon me. It's a special feeling I'll never forget.

Now I choose to love. It says in 1 Corinthians that if I don't have love, I have nothing. God is love, so we should be love. At this point in my life, I seek first the Kingdom of God in everything I do. There's so much being added to my life. I now have more peace, a car, the best job I have ever had, and I've moved into my own place. I stay active in my church, which I believe is important, because I learn more about who I am in God there. I lived for myself for so long, but I'm learning how to live for Jesus and to love others.

[Gold]

I believe heaven will be a place of complete peace and eternal life with my King, Jesus. I also think Jesus didn't just die for us to say a prayer to go to heaven. He died so we can live for Him here on earth and enjoy a relationship with Him now.

[Final Thoughts]

I used to think I didn't matter and I was worthless. I believed the enemy's lies for so long it almost killed me. The truth is, we all matter, and we all have a purpose through Jesus Christ. To think that the Creator of the never-ending universe took the time to create you is mind blowing. You were made for a purpose, so live with a purpose. Be uniquely you to reach people like you!

words of [WISDOM]

Trey's Life Verse

"I love the Lord, for he heard my voice; he heard my cry for mercy. Because he turned his ear to me, I will call on him as long as I live. The cords of death entangled me, the anguish of the grave came over me; I was overcome by distress and sorrow. Then I called on the name of the Lord: "Lord, save me!" The Lord is gracious and righteous; our God is full of compassion. The Lord protects the unwary; when I was brought low, he saved me. Return to your rest, my soul, for the Lord has been good to you. For you, Lord, have delivered me from death, my eyes from tears, my feet from stumbling, that I may walk before the Lord in the land of the living. I trusted in the Lord when I said, "I am greatly afflicted."

Psalm 116:1-10

Roger's Story

[Gray]

I grew up in a home in the projects with five brothers and sisters. My dad was a Korean War veteran. I'm not sure what he experienced over there, but he drank heavily to try and deal with the nightmares. His PTSD, Post-Traumatic Stress Disorder, (known as "shell shock" back then) wasn't treated effectively. I loved my dad and always wanted to make him happy.

Although we didn't have much, I never saw myself as any different than anyone else. Using humor to overcome my natural insecurities, I was the class-clown always trying to get a laugh. This helped me get the attention and acceptance that all kids desire.

As far as church attendance goes, my family was CEO: Christmas and Easter Only. Eventually, a church bus began coming by to pick me and my siblings up. Brother Galloway and Ms. Shortreed were wonderful people who loved God and loved people. I enjoyed going to church, but I didn't really have a personal relationship with Jesus.

Through Junior High and High School I avoided using drugs and rarely drank alcohol. My senior year I was hanging out with some friends one afternoon in one of their bedrooms. One guy was smoking some weed and offered it to me. When I hesitated he said, "Don't worry about it, Bro. This stuff just makes you relax. It doesn't make you do anything stupid." He immediately leaned forward in his chair and spit onto the screen of an open window. His nasty spit hung there, clinging disgustingly to the screen. I thought to myself, "Yeah, dude. Nothing stupid at all!"

It was like a sign that I shouldn't touch the stuff. Young and dumb, I ignored the warning and gave it a shot. I was soon regularly drinking alcohol and smoking weed and cigarettes. This put me in a group of friends who had the same habits reinforcing my bad behavior.

A little while later, I met the love of my life and we got married. She didn't approve of my drug use, so I hid it from her. We had our first child, and I felt conflicted about my substance abuse. Using marijuana and alcohol lowered my inhibitions and made me feel better about myself. I had no desire to quit, but I wanted to take my family to church. So I figured I could do both, and we began going to church regularly.

[Red]

I began to feel guilty about my alcohol and drug use the more I attended church. I excused my actions by pointing to others who smoked cigarettes and still went to church. I told myself there were hypocrites in every church. While those thoughts gave me an excuse, I knew deep down I wasn't living the way I should be. Most of the people at church were very friendly and loving, which only added to my guilt.

One of the main reasons addictions are so hard to break is because it's easy to justify your actions to yourself when you're tempted. I realize now that I just wanted to be accepted and loved for who I was. The substances just made it easier to feel better about myself and mask my insecurities. God knew this, and He brought me to my breaking point one Sunday morning.

[White]

As I sat in church, a feeling washed over me. I felt the love, conviction, and power of God fall upon my soul. At the end of the sermon I went forward. Crying tears of repentance, I acknowledged Jesus as my Lord and my Savior. It was a moment I'll never forget. I had never felt such peace and joy throughout my whole being. My wife was so happy. We celebrated together and began talking about my baptism.

[Blue]

I talked to the pastor about what baptism means. He explained it all very clearly to me. The day of my baptism was special. I was happy all of my family could be there. I had always wanted to be a good example for my kids, and I was proud as I stood before my church and family being obedient to the teaching of Jesus to be baptized. I decided to give up drugs after my salvation. In my heart, I knew it wasn't something my wife or Jesus wanted me doing.

[Green]

I got heavily involved in my church. I became a greeter and helped lead Awana activities for the kids. I began going to lunch after church every week with my pastors. For the first few weeks and months after my salvation, I stayed away from drugs. Eventually though, I made excuses and justified to myself how using drugs occasionally would be okay. Of course, 'occasionally' turned into 'regularly'.

I got a new job and met the man who would introduce me to cocaine. This was a game changer! Cocaine became what I lived for. It gave me energy that was off the charts. Looking back, I realize the best part of using cocaine was the sheer excitement of knowing I was going to get my fix.

I had always wanted to work in radio, and I finally got my big break. I was hired by one of the most popular radio stations in my home state. This opened lots of doors for me and drugs were the fuel for my career rise.

Being a functioning drug addict was easy for me. In my mind, I used it to help me have the courage to perform my duties at my dream job. I still loved God, church, and my family, but cocaine gave me the high I needed to thrive.

Like they say, "All good things must come to an end." I lost my beloved job at the radio station. It was a cruel blow, but I handled it the best way I knew how...stoned. I bounced around from job to job, always hoping for another break. Drugs and alcohol remained part of my everyday life.

I was able to stay relevant in the industry, getting a few small radio gigs here and there. My drug use got worse. I remember my daily routine would be to wake up in the morning and take a hit of coke to get going. I would then use alcohol and weed throughout the day and evening. At bedtime, I would swig some NyQuil to get some sleep. The next morning, I would begin the same unhealthy cycle all over again.

Finally, my wife came to her breaking point. She gave me an ultimatum: My family or my drugs. I knew without a doubt she meant it.

I signed up with Bridgeway, a rehab clinic, for their 28 day outpatient program and joined Alcoholics Anonymous. My new daily routine was much different than the old one. I would go to work, then an AA meeting at lunch, back to work, then Bridgeway sessions after work, then home to my wife.

I cannot put into words the encouragement, patience, devotion, and love my amazing wife displayed to me throughout our relationship. It wasn't easy to give up my addictions but something special replaced them. My relationship with God became real again. As incredible as my wife was to me, God proved himself faithful as well. He showed true grace and forgiveness to me, a sinner. I know I'm not worthy of His love, and I never will be, but He loves me anyway.

It says in the Bible that God will give you the desires of your heart. I know it's true. Just after I got clean, an unexpected opportunity came up for me to go back into a major radio position. This time, I got to do it sober. Another amazing opportunity came up a few years later. I had the chance to be in the movie "Antiquities". It was a dream come true for me to be cast in a Hollywood movie. I felt like it was something my family could really be proud of me doing.

Life has its challenges, but I'm happy to say I've been sober for 13 years. I get to work with some amazing people, and I enjoy what I do. I found out about a program called "Meals on wheels". They deliver food to people who don't have enough to eat. I serve there weekly and it's such a blessing to help others. Many of the people we help can't get around well. They light up when we show up with a package. I think they enjoy the fellowship almost as much as the food. We get to talk and laugh which is just as special for me as it is for them.

It fills me with joy to say all of my kids are followers of Jesus. There are many decisions I regret, but knowing God drew my kids to salvation in spite of my actions makes me love Him even more. I love my kids, and I'm proud of them all.

I want to be sure to keep this testimony real. The truth is sometimes I still blow it. Not with drugs or alcohol. My wife and I agreed I wasn't allowed a relapse. Well, she told me I wasn't allowed one, and I don't want to test her. But I can get angry. I can be a jerk. Road rage sneaks up on everyone, right? I'm working on my patience. I never claim to be perfect, because I'm not. But I try every day to follow Christ. The one thing I never want to do is to deny Jesus. With my words and my actions, I want to always acknowledge Him as my Savior.

God took a drug-addicted, alcoholic and turned him into a Bible believing, hope-filled, Jesus loving, joyful man. I read my Bible daily and I've even gone to church by myself when my wife was sick. Those are big wins for me. I'm still a work in progress. I'm humbled to even call myself a child of God, but that's what He calls me, so that is what I am!

[Gold]

Heaven? That's a good question. I look forward to seeing my dad. Later in life he turned his life around. I think we'll enjoy each other a lot. Knowing that my wife and kids will be there is exciting. Seeing Jesus will be awesome! It's hard to imagine how cool that will be. I think heaven will be peaceful — no more mean emails or texts. There's so much turmoil in the world. It will be nice to all get along for a change.

[Final Thoughts]

I want people to know there is hope. No matter how bad things may seem, don't give up. Don't ever believe there isn't a way out of your situation. Ask God to help you, and do your part in the process.

words of [WISDOM]

"Recovery is hard. Regret is harder."
- Brittany Burgunder

"And the God of all grace, who called you to his eternal glory in Christ,
after you have suffered a little while,
will himself restore you and make you strong, firm and steadfast."
- Peter, one of Jesus' disciples
1 Peter 5:10

"Our greatest glory is not in never failing, but in rising up every time we fail."
- Ralph Waldo Emerson

Sarah's Story

[Gray]

I was raised in a wonderful Christian home and had the most loving parents. All of my family seemed to know the Lord in a way that I didn't. When I was seven, I asked Jesus into my heart and then again early in my teenage years, but I never truly meant it. It was more of an emotional moment without any real life change.

When you aren't grounded in a relationship with Jesus or the truth of the Bible, anything can become your identity. My emotions ruled me, and I lived life for myself. The enemy used my lack of identity as a stronghold in my life. I struggled with my sexual identity, first with confused emotions towards boys and then by acting on feelings towards girls.

Since my family didn't approve of this, I felt rejected by them and in turn by God. There was a day in high school when I felt especially confused and alone. I left school, took a large dose of Tylenol P.M. and started aimlessly driving around. My mom got word I wasn't at school and began searching for me. On a desolate back road, she prayed, "God, please help me find Sarah." Suddenly she saw my car! She sped up. I saw her following me, so I pulled over. I almost collapsed when I got out of the car.

My mom rushed me to the hospital, quickly getting me the care I needed. I was soon transferred to a mental facility for a week. I received tons of letters and felt love from those who visited me, but my low self-esteem didn't allow me to embrace their love. I told myself they only felt sorry for me.

After I graduated high school, I decided to move out of town to go to college and play softball. My rebellious lifestyle didn't change. I would drink and smoke weed every night and really party on the weekends. Not surprisingly, I failed a few classes. When my mom found out about my grades and lifestyle, she gave me an ultimatum to straighten up or be cut off financially. She said I was living against the Word of God and she wouldn't fund it.

I called up an old boyfriend from high school to see if he wanted to get high. One thing led to another and I got pregnant with my daughter,

69

Emery. I came home from college and got a job as a waitress. On a positive note, being pregnant gave me a healthy sense of purpose.

After Emery was born, I continued to wait tables and decided to go to school to become a surgical technologist. This environment turned out to be toxic for me. I had enough cash in my pocket to drink and smoke nightly after work, but would lie to my parents telling them I was working late and tips were bad. My unhealthy relationships continued as well. When I would get with someone, I would do anything I could to hold onto them. I wanted to be loved so badly.

I was selfish. I had a little girl at home longing to see her mommy, but most of the time, I wouldn't go home. We even had a family friend, Melissa, who helped raise Emery, because I was out partying. What an incredible blessing Melissa turned out to be. I still look back on all of this with shame and guilt.

I ended up getting into another relationship with a woman who used methamphetamine. I didn't know she was using meth when we met, but I didn't leave when I found out. Of course, I ended up trying meth. It destroyed me. This particular relationship made me feel worthless with constant verbal, physical, and emotional abuse. I clung to it though. Satan had fooled me into believing that I wasn't worth anything more than this.

We had a fight, and I went to a friend's house. While I was staying there, I found some checks in her closet. I forged them for $1000. Eventually I was arrested for forgery. I was released the same night, because it was my first offense.

On another night, I was staying at an old house used for selling drugs. I had been up for days, so I passed out on an old love seat without a cushion on it. The cold, drafty house didn't have any heat, and it was the middle of winter. Waking up by myself, I looked down and saw a needle hanging out of my arm. I remember praying to God to do something, to please take me out of this mess if there was any chance of me living a better life.

A little while later, my girlfriend showed up with her ex-boyfriend to take me home. As we pulled into the driveway, three police cars pulled in and I was arrested and stayed in jail for a while this time. God was answering my prayer, but I didn't realize it at the time.

After 30 days, I finally convinced my mom to bail me out of jail. She agreed with me that it would look good to a judge if I went to a rehab program voluntarily. This would give me a better chance of avoiding prison. My mom bailed me out of jail for $1500 and paid $1000 for me to go to rehab. I left the rehab program within an hour. I called everyone I could to try to get a ride. As I sat on the curb, I had time to think about what I had just done to my mom. I realized in that moment how horrible of a person I had become.

Other terribly abusive things happened to me, and I thought about killing myself. My daughter, Emery, would come to my mind, and I knew I couldn't go through with it. After a long time, I finally got fed up with the life I was living.

[Red]

Several months after my arrest I remember crying out to God. I told Him I was tired, that I didn't know how else to live life, and how I needed His help. Then one day, I was sitting outside after a Narcotics Anonymous meeting, and I was really upset with the way my life had turned out. A guy walked over to me and sat down. He asked me what was wrong. I told him. He started to talk to me about the Lord. This caught my attention. He told me about a place called "The Father's House." It was a six-month long, faith-based rehab program. I felt a tug on my broken heart, and I took the chance being offered to me. I felt something I hadn't felt in a very long time: hope. So I went, and I stayed. It wasn't easy, but God broke me down bit by bit. Then He slowly built me back up.

He stripped away from me everything that wasn't of Him and then put the desire to know Him in my heart. It took me time to surrender. About three months into my stay at the Father's House, I was burdened by my desire for other people's approval. Finally, walking across the campus, I knew it was time to surrender.

[White]

I walked into the empty sanctuary, knelt down at the altar, and broke down. Sobbing to God, I cried out for Him to take over. I may have asked Jesus into my heart a few times before in my life, but I know, in that moment, on that altar, is when God became the Lord of my life. A peace flooded my soul like never before. From that time on, I have lived and longed only for God's approval.

colors of salvation

[Blue]

At the writing of this book, I'm planning on getting baptized, but the COVID-19 virus has closed our church building for a few weeks. I'm excited to be publicly baptized with my family and friends there.

[Green]

God opened my eyes and my heart to a lot of things while I was at The Father's House. He showed me all of the people in my life who had been praying hard for me and where others had stood in the gap while I was away from Emery. He showed me His love through all of these people. He made me a new creation. He gave me a new heart.

My family never stopped praying for me. I know there were times they wanted to give up, but they didn't. It was tough for them to be obedient and cut me off completely — to allow me to move alone into total darkness. But their obedience to God allowed me to see the light of Jesus in the darkness. I finally found my true identity and my purpose. My identity is that I am a child of God, and my purpose is to live for Jesus Christ. There is no greater joy than this.

God took everything from me, so all I had was Him. He redeemed my soul. He restored me to my family. He has given me blessing on top of blessing, even though I don't deserve it. He gave me the most wonderful, godly husband who I met while recovering in The Father's House. Charlie has a similar story to mine. He never pursued me while we were at the Father's House together. He showed me Christ's love, and he waited patiently for me.

Charlie didn't want to come between me and the time I needed to spend building my relationship with Jesus. He knew I needed time to heal. He's everything I ever dreamed of in a spouse. I never truly loved someone romantically until I loved Charlie. I am so grateful for this new life the Lord has given me.

I am so grateful for my family. My mom is the strongest person I know. She raised Emery while I was gone, during a time when my dad was extremely sick and near death. They made sure Emery felt loved and adored. They brought her up in the Lord and always did what was best for her. I'm grateful for the hard decisions they made, keeping me from Emery when they knew it would bring her harm. I know their faith and love for

God is what the Lord used to bring me to Jesus. It's nothing short of a miracle. I am a miracle.

[Gold]

When I think of what heaven will be like I think of the Mercy Me song "I Can Only Imagine". I'm not sure how I'll react to seeing Jesus, only that it will be incredible — no more pain, no more suffering — only joy, peace, and worshiping our King!

[Final Thoughts]

If you seek the Lord and seek Him with your whole heart, you WILL find Him. That's one of His promises to us. He never breaks a promise. There is no greater joy in this world than when you find the Lord.

words of [HOPE]

"May the God of hope fill you with all joy and peace as you trust in him,
so that you may overflow with hope by the power of the Holy Spirit."
Romans 15:13

Being a mom of an addict is tough. My daughter's problems started in middle school as she felt like she didn't fit in. She was trying to find her place in life and was looking in all the wrong places. Satan knows right where to attack us and where we are vulnerable. If you are a follower of Christ, you have God's Word to battle against the enemy and the armor of God to protect you. Prayer is powerful. I would often prayerfully sing "I Cast All My Cares Upon You" by David Kocijan:

I cast all my cares upon You
I lay all of my burdens down at Your feet
And any time I don't know what to do
I will cast all my cares upon You
I will cast all my cares upon You

My husband and I struggled with the balance between loving and enabling her. I learned to take things day by day and pray for wisdom. There were times I wanted to give up. One day I remember reading my Bible and the words seemed to leap off the page. "The Lord will fight for you; you need only to be still." (Exodus 14:14)

God is faithful! My daughter has been clean for three years and is a miracle. She loves the Lord her God with all her heart, soul, mind and strength. There is power in prayer!

Brenda Hart
Proud Mom of Sarah

Rikki's Story

[Gray]

I was born in Honolulu, Hawaii. My mom gave me up for adoption to a family who was stationed there in the Air Force. They already had two kids of their own, and I was happy to have a brother and sister to play with growing up.

At the age of two, we moved away from my homeland of Hawaii. This was the first of many, many moves for me. I was raised a true military brat. This caused me and my siblings to become really close, because we couldn't develop close friendships with other kids in such a short amount of time.

From as far back as I can remember, I believed there was a God. I never really doubted He was out there somewhere watching over me. We almost always went to church wherever we lived. My dad was Catholic and my mom was Baptist. We always went to a Baptist Church. I enjoyed going to church and found most people there were really nice.

[Red]

We were living in a subdivision when I was in elementary school. We hadn't found a church yet. Some people from a local church would drive their church bus to our neighborhood on Saturdays. They would talk about Jesus to everyone who were out riding their bikes or walking around. They were very kind and friendly people.

One man stopped me on my bike to talk with me. He explained that the Bible teaches everyone has sinned. Because we are sinners, we need a Savior. Then he told me how Jesus came to earth and lived a perfect life, died to take my sins away, and conquered death by rising up from the tomb to live again. Now, because of the sacrifice Jesus made, we can be right with God. We can't earn it. It's a gift God gives us.

[White]

All of this made sense to me and I prayed right there with him for salvation. I gladly acknowledged Jesus as my Lord while talking with this man. Honestly, I didn't feel a huge difference. I already believed in God,

75

and while it made sense to acknowledge him as my Lord and Savior, it wasn't a huge change in the way I understood my life or my faith.

I have heard people share their testimony about how they experienced an overwhelming moment of realizing who Jesus is, but I didn't have those feelings. Maybe it was because I was young. I did however experience a sense of peace inside, and I was happy to be known as a Christian.

A little while later, my brother and our friend rode up on their bikes. The man told them about Jesus too. He asked us if we wanted to ride their bus to church the next day. It sounded fun to us, so we introduced him to our parents and got their permission. They agreed to let us go, and we began riding the church bus regularly.

While my parents liked the idea of us going to church, they weren't interested in always going themselves. I think to them, church was a religion that taught people right from wrong, more than a dynamic personal relationship with Jesus.

My brother and our friend also got saved over the next few weeks. We continued to go to this church regularly and really enjoyed it. I wonder sometimes why more people in church these days don't go out and tell people about Jesus. Eventually we had to move again and I said goodbye to my church friends.

[Blue]

Over the next few years we moved several times. At about the age of 14, my brother, our cousin's husband, Charlie, and I got really involved in a new church we were attending in a new town. We got into some deep discussions about God, which were really interesting to me. My brother and Charlie decided to get baptized. I'm not really sure why I didn't get baptized when I got saved. Maybe it was because I was so young or because my parents didn't go to that church often. But, for whatever reason, I had not been baptized and I knew I wanted and needed to be.

Our pastor at this church talked to us several times about being baptized. He asked us questions about why we needed to be baptized and had us explain what the Bible teaches about it. The day of our baptism was exciting. Most of our family was there, but my dad could not make it. I walked into the water and our pastor introduced me to the church. I remember he put his foot on top of both of my feet when he went to dunk me under the water. I guess that was to give him a better grip, so he wouldn't drop me. Being baptized energized me in my faith. I wasn't perfect or anything, but I was a pretty good kid.

[Green]

My spiritual life was hot and cold over the next few years. The first time I tried smoking weed with some friends of mine, it did absolutely nothing for me. I'm not even sure it was really marijuana. I felt nothing.

Later, in high school, I would get together with some of my friends to jam out on our guitars. They had the real stuff. It never seemed like a big deal when I got high with them. I would do it with my friends and not worry about using again until we got together to jam. For some reason we never touched alcohol. I wouldn't try alcohol until later in life, and it affected me in a totally different way than marijuana did.

All through Junior High and High School I dated this beautiful redheaded girl named Teresa. I had never liked redheads before her, but she was different. We fell in love and got married when I was twenty.

We soon had kids and enjoyed being a family. I had not done drugs in several years and we were regularly going to church. During this time we were very active in our church. We went on Sunday mornings and evenings, Wednesday nights, and to Thursday night visitation. Our life revolved around church activities. We figured it was good for us and good for our kids to be in church.

We moved and decided to intentionally look for a small church to join. We thought it would be good to go to a church where we would know everyone and build close friendships. We found one we liked with a pastor who taught good biblical sermons. After attending there for a little while, the pastor asked to speak with me alone. Being Hawaiian, my hair was long, black, and thick. He explained to me that some of the members didn't like my long hair, and he asked me if I would consider cutting it. That was the last time we went there.

In my late twenties, Teresa and I went to a bar with some of her coworkers. They wanted me to do a shot of alcohol with them. We had a fun evening. Alcohol became a part of our social life. It escalated quickly, and I discovered I wasn't able to control it. When I began drinking I would drink until I passed out. There wasn't a stop button for me with alcohol.

I had a nagging knee injury from racing the church van home on my 10-speed when I was younger. An added benefit from drinking alcohol was my knee pain was numbed. This gave me a good excuse to drink regularly.

In my early 30's, I went to a new doctor who prescribed me a new pain medicine for my knee. It relieved the pain without the awful side effects and hangovers of alcohol. I quit drinking immediately. Spiritually and emotionally, it made me feel better to not get drunk daily.

After I turned 40, my doctor wanted me to stop taking the prescription meds for my knee. I began drinking again, and this time it got much worse. I would begin drinking and wake up the next morning with empty bottles of alcohol laying around my bed that I didn't remember drinking.

We moved into a new home. My neighbor invited me to go to church with him. I was hesitant because of past hurts at churches, and I knew I wasn't living right. Over the next few weeks, Jesus gently drew me back into fellowship with other believers. It was refreshing to be back in church. A little while later I had knee surgery, and my pain was totally relieved. Praise the Lord!

I gave up alcohol and restored my walk with Jesus. While life hasn't been easy, I know God loves me and that I love him. I'm still trying to learn more about God and follow him better. I am thankful he loves me even when I struggle to follow him.

[Gold]

I believe heaven will be a place where there is no more pain. Having experienced physical pain most of my life, this sounds amazing. I look forward to seeing loved ones who have gone before me. It's hard for me to imagine how wonderful heaven will truly be.

[Final Thoughts]

I want people who hear my story to know there is hope for you. No matter how bad you think you are, Jesus can forgive and restore you. He can make things even better than you can imagine!

words of [WISDOM]

An estimated 88,000 people die from alcohol-related causes each year.[4]

Alcohol is the third leading preventable cause of death in the United States. [4]

"Do not get drunk on wine, which leads to debauchery.
Instead, be filled with the Spirit,"
- Paul the Apostle
Ephesians 5:18

In 2010, alcohol abuse cost the United States $249 billion.[4]

Sybil's Story

[Gray]

I was born to a praying mother and a drinking father. My parents taught me and my three siblings respect early on in life through fear. They taught us to believe phrases like, "I brought you into this world and I can take you out" and "Children are to be seen, not heard."

My parents raised the four of us children to live the American dream. Both of my parents were educated and they bought their own home. My dad worked while my mother was a stay-at-home mom. She stayed busy taking care of the house and children.

We were in church regularly. We weren't allowed to wear pants or listen to secular music. We ate every meal at the kitchen table. Dad sat at the head of the table. Every morning he raised his half pint of whisky and announced, "I drink my breakfast". We always said grace before eating and asked to be excused from the table before leaving.

Every Saturday, my father and brother cut the yard and washed the cars. The girls washed clothes and hung them up on the line in the back yard to dry. Mother required all of us to take music lessons. The girls also took classes in proper etiquette, and our brother worked on cars with our dad.

We were constantly subject to bloody beatings for the smallest of infractions. Things like leaving the bread wrapper untied would result in a beating. When I went to school people thought I was snobby, but actually I was in pain and working hard to keep people from seeing my marks. Other than the insanity in my home, I was very sheltered.

By the age of nine years old, I knew how to gage how much my father had drank. At half-a-pint he was happy and engaging. A whole pint led to him wanting our family to go for a ride with him. Inevitably, on the second pint, somebody did something wrong, upsetting him. Two-and-a-half pints in, we were lined up to be whipped with an electric extension cord. This was something we did not discuss outside of the house — ever.

This type of rearing does not foster empowered children. As a child of an alcoholic, I learned survival skills. Mine were making straight A's in school and making sure every household chore was done with perfection. I made sure to keep my three younger siblings in line.

Some of my survival skills proved to serve me well. I graduated from Central High School and attended the University of Central Arkansas on an academic scholarship. When I graduated, I moved to California at 21. By the age of 25, I had my own business, purchased a $300,000 home, and collected original art. I was single with no children, but I had a group of like-minded friends to spend my time with.

On weekends I smoked weed and listened to jazz music. I would go out with my friends dancing, horseback riding, and traveling. I was having the time of my life. One day, I was on my way to a business appointment when I was abducted! Some guys had been randomly abducting women in my town. By the end of the encounter I was completely shattered.

I had two female acquaintances — who I had gotten high with in the past — come visit me, and they realized how broken I was. They assisted me with a bath, combed my hair, and fed me. Unfortunately, behind my back, they called a drug dealer who had wanted to meet me. He gave me drugs masking all of the pain, shame, and terror I felt. I was immediately addicted and asked him to move in with me. In a month, I went from being a successful business woman to living to get high all day, every day.

[Red]

Having been raised in church, I knew about God, but I had never had a real relationship with Him. At my lowest point I weighed 97 pounds, all of my hair had fallen out, and I had lost everything. Not only did I lose all my stuff, but the most important thing to me: the proud way my mom looked at me. I had changed from the one who fixed problems in our family to one who was like a tornado destroying the lives of others. I went from being the golden child to the black sheep of the family.

I no longer lived, I just existed. I hated mirrors, no longer recognizing my pitiful reflection and devastated by it. I hated my life and myself. I decided the best thing I could do was die. This would end the pain and shame of my family. I cleaned my house spotless, bathed, did my hair, applied makeup flawlessly, and wrote letters to each of my loved ones.

I set off insect poison foggers all around me and went to sleep, believing my fight was over. Hours later, I woke up shocked and sick. I had read the label saying it could be fatal, and thought they were much more lethal.

In a place of hopeless darkness I met Jesus. The Good Shepherd personally left the 99 and came for me. I was sick, and my choices in my addiction were killing me. That is when I knew in the depths of soul Jesus was and is the Great Physician. I was drowning in self-loathing when I was redeemed.

[White]

I had gone into residential treatment on several occasions, for many different reasons. I was on my way to treatment again, but this time I knew I could no longer survive on this path. I was completely bankrupt mentally, physically, and spiritually. I said a simple prayer.

On the car ride, I looked out the window and saw the blue sky, bellowing clouds, and a gentle breeze moving through the leaves on the trees. I whispered, "Jesus, I have nothing left, but pain, shame, and breath. If you will take this pain and shame, I will give you my breath." He took them and my sins away.

[Blue]

I had been baptized as a teenager. After much prayer I felt like God was pleased with my walk with Him. The Bible verse from Luke 7:47-48 holds a special place in my heart, "Therefore, I tell you, her many sins have been forgiven — as her great love has shown. But whoever has been forgiven little loves little." Then Jesus said to her, "Your sins are forgiven."

[Green]

I kept my word to use my breath for Jesus. I've used my breath to carry his message of redemption all over the nation on many platforms, such as recruiting for and working with minority congregations for the Ecumenical AIDS Ministry in Atlanta, Georgia; the Presbyterian Conference in Newark, New Jersey; and the Baptist Southern Convention in colleges and universities all over the state of Arkansas. It's through Jesus opening these doors of ministry that I have been able to serve.

The more time I spent seeking Jesus in the Bible, devotionals, and prayer, the more He revealed Himself to me. I started sleeping peacefully and rising with hope. My vision changed. I didn't just see the wreckage of my past, but now I also saw His blessings. I heard the birds singing in the morning. I saw the gift of love from my incredible husband, Bobby. I felt the blessings of being a mom to my boys, Jovon, Rodney, and Raphael. My sweet mother seemed to breathe again. I was reborn.

My mother had traveled the world doing missionary work until she retired. When she came to a church where I was preaching, she got up and said, "I see God! I stand here looking at a miracle."

My sisters were in awe of my transformed life, going from being lost in addiction to living boldly for Jesus in recovery. My addiction affected my parents, siblings, husband, and children. Both of my parents' journeys ended in this life with me by their side, saved and sober. All of our lives have been enriched and set on a different path because we can celebrate my recovery.

In the 26 years that I have been saved, sober, and redeemed, a lot has happened. I've received my training at the University of Arkansas Medical Sciences in Clinical Pastoral Education and became a Chaplain. I have graduated from a school of ministry, and I am now a licensed and ordained minister. I have had the privilege of being awarded millions of dollars of grant money for substance abuse prevention. I now work for a community healthcare clinic. I also now get the awesome privilege of serving as a leader at Celebrate Recovery in our church.

My walk with God has changed everything. I am not alone. I am loved greatly. My house has been adopted into the family of God.

When I first got sober and based my life on faith, my routine was to begin each day with prayer and meditation, take my boys to daycare, go to work, pick them up, prepare and serve dinner at the kitchen table with my family, and then go to a recovery meeting. I stayed busy.

Three months into this daily routine, my eldest son looked at me and asked, "Are you coming back for me?" I went to my sponsor crying. I exclaimed, "It's been three months!! I am doing everything I am supposed to do and he still asks me if I am coming back!"

My sponsor said, "You don't get a brownie button because you are doing what you are supposed to do. Just keep coming back for him." I did!

When he was 16 his car broke down. He was overwhelmed by the speeding cars passing by, people blowing their horn at him, and the complete lack of compassion by anyone seeing him broken down on the side of the road. He didn't know what to do, so he called me. I told him to close his eyes, take a slow deep breath in and out, and then to open his eyes and tell me what he sees. He saw a Goodyear sign. I called the company and got everything handled from my office downtown. I still left and drove across town to him to insure his well-being. When I arrived he was watching TV.

He turned around and said, "Hi, mom."

I replied, "Hi, mom? Aren't you surprised to see me?"

Jovon answered, "No. I knew you would come for me."

By God's grace that is a picture of recovery! A picture of a new life! Our boys are great young men now, with homes of their own (Praise Jesus!). They have married, giving us two beautiful daughters-in-law. We also now have a grandson and another one on the way. None of that would exist for me without my recovery in Jesus. Life still has its mountains and valleys, but God has provided the tools, fellowship, and purpose for me to remain sober through Celebrate Recovery in my church. I'm able to use my experiences, good and bad, to help others!

[Gold]

In Heaven, we will be in the presence of Jesus and the perfect place He has prepared for us. We'll get to learn and hear Jesus teach. We'll get to attend wonderful worship services. Families will be reconciled. We will get to work, but it will be work we enjoy, and it will be fulfilling for us.

[Final Thoughts]

The enemy comes to kill, steal and destroy. He does this through things we think will be fun, but lead to our misery. Jesus gives us true joy that never ends and gives us abundant life.

words of [WISDOM]

Your Pain can become your Purpose.
Your Test can become your Testimony.
Your Mistakes can become your Mission!
-Anonymous

"What gives me the most hope every day is God's grace; knowing that his grace is going to give me the strength for whatever I face, knowing that nothing is a surprise to God."
- Rick Warren

"Oft hope is born when all is forlorn."
- J.R.R. Tolkien

John Ryan's Story

[Gray]

My family was like most everyone else's that I knew growing up. Dad had a good job and worked hard. Mom loved and cared for me and my little sister. Dad wasn't religious. Mom was Catholic, so we went to Mass on Christmas and Easter. This was about the only time Jesus was discussed in our family. It wasn't until I was in my late teens that I realized my mom and dad had alcohol problems. They hid it well.

When I was in the eighth grade I hung out with my older cousin whenever I could. I thought he was cool, and I wanted to be just like him. He drank and smoked weed regularly, so I jumped at the chance to try it when he offered. My two best friends had older brothers who also smoked marijuana. We began drinking and smoking weed on the weekends. In the ninth grade, I tried meth for the first time. What a rush! I loved it from the start. Little did I know how miserable it would end up making me.

I was gifted athletically. In high school I was one of the best all-around athletes in our program. I was the starting quarterback on our football team, catcher on the baseball team, shooting guard in basketball, and placed second in state in the hurdles all while doing meth every weekend. By my senior year, I was using meth daily, and I dropped out of school.

I found a job at a local lumberyard. Drugs were expensive. It became unbearable to wait on my paycheck to get a fix, so I began dealing drugs to afford my habit. At the age of 20, I began cooking meth. I partied hard with lots of drugs, sex, and alcohol. The highs were sky high, and the lows were incredibly low.

Not surprisingly, I got a girl pregnant. We had a son. Both of us were strung out. We were terrible parents. Our relationship didn't last long. I began racking up criminal charges over the next three years. When I was 23, I wrecked my truck. Unfortunately, I had a meth lab in the back of the truck and got four felony charges. I was sent to jail. While there, I sobered up and realized I was living wrong. I knew there was a better life than the one I was living. When I got out of jail, I went straight to rehab.

After getting out of rehab, I was going to a Narcotics Anonymous meeting when I ran into the little sister of one of my friends. I was always attracted to Brooke when we were young, so I asked her out. She said she probably shouldn't, because she had heard about me getting busted. But against her better judgment she relented and agreed to go out with me. We hit it off and within a month she was pregnant. I wasn't upset. I was actually very happy to be with her and we got married.

Even though I was smoking weed, drinking alcohol, and taking Xanax regularly, I considered myself sober, because I wasn't using meth. Brooke had our son. When he was a few months old my ex-girlfriend asked if we could watch my other child for about three hours. Three hours turned into three years. Brooke was immediately the mother of my two kids, and it was incredibly hard on her and our new marriage.

[Red]

Brooke wanted to go to church, so we went. I still got high regularly, but I enjoyed going to church. At first I didn't really listen a lot, but the people there seemed very nice. When I did begin listening, a lot of the things they taught didn't make any sense to me. I was a total skeptic. I had a lot of doubts about what they taught and even laughed at some of the ideas they believed. It seemed so ridiculous that they believed there was a God who would love me without Him getting something in return.

I began noticing there was something different about certain people in the church. At first I thought they were faking it, being so happy and friendly. But, as time went by, I realized there was something fundamentally different about them.

Josh Turner, a pastor there, was one of those people. His wife, Crystal, was pregnant. They seemed like really good people. When she had their little girl, the child had SMA, which is a rare, deadly disease. I watched Josh over the next couple of months, while his new baby was in the hospital, and it was amazing. He was hurting, and I could tell it was tough, but he had peace in the storm. I didn't understand it. When things would go bad in my life I would blow up. When his little girl passed away, Josh still had that sense of peace even though he was mourning the loss of his child. I wanted what he had.

On a Sunday night service, God got my attention. There was something unique about that service. Our lead Pastor, Jason Tallent, was teaching from the book of Revelation. I was hanging on every word. I was feeling something inside of me wanting to know Jesus, to change and follow Him. It was all making perfect sense to me. I didn't hesitate when he finished preaching and gave the altar call. Excitedly, I went forward. I prayed for salvation with Pastor Jason and Josh. I felt reborn down in my soul.

[Blue]

I was excited to get baptized. I wanted to obey Jesus. My oldest son, Jace, had also acknowledged Jesus as his Lord. We got baptized on the same day. It was a great day.

[Green]

I went to work and started telling everyone about my new relationship with Jesus. They just laughed at me. About a month later I got fired. This wasn't going the way I thought it would. Jesus was supposed to fix all of my problems and make me a new person who people respected, not have people laugh at me and lose my job.

I got another job. On my first day there, the guy I was working with used meth on our break. Feeling bold I told him about how I used to do drugs but had gotten saved. I didn't have any idea of how to share Jesus to him, but I passionately tried. A few months later life got hard. Brooke and I were always fighting. We had too many bills, kids, and activities going on. God hadn't fixed everything the way I thought He would. In my mind, I was supposed to have it all together like those church people. I didn't.

I was assigned to a job site where I was again working with the guy who had used meth in front of me the prior month. I asked him for a hit. He gave me a hard time for preaching to him and now asking for drugs. I didn't care. After 10 years clean from meth I fell hard. Within a week, I was dealing again.

Life was overwhelming. I was on several athletic committees at our local school, volunteered in our churches kids program, and Brooke was expecting our fourth child. My relapse was bad. I was on a path of destruction. I got a hold of some heroine, and I was hooked. I had a $400-a-day drug habit. Brooke was beginning to question me about using, but I lied and denied.

I got another felony charge and Brooke left me. I was laying on the couch worn out, broke, and miserable. Brooke came home from being gone with the kids all weekend. She offered to help get me into a rehab facility. Half of me hated the thought of going to rehab. The other half knew I was headed to prison or death without it. It was a battle in my very soul, but I finally agreed to go to a place Brooke had found for me.

The Father's House is a Christian based rehab program. It was a long drive out to their facility. We arrived and I got checked in. It broke my heart to watch Brooke leave.

Detoxing was painful. But once the drugs were out of my system my mind became incredibly clear. I wanted to get clean and stay clean. I realized I loved Brooke, my family, and Jesus more than any high could ever give me. The Bible began to make sense in ways I had never experienced. I decided I would follow the teachings of Jesus, no matter the cost, and I would become the man God created me to be. No excuses.

When I got out of rehab, I got rid of every bad influence in my life, including friends who I knew would drag me down. I was focused, and Brooke could see the difference. We reconciled and agreed to put God 100% in charge of our marriage and family.

I got a job building carports. A little while later, I began to feel like God wanted me to start my own business. It wasn't easy, but He blessed me, and I now own a successful business installing metal buildings. My business was doing pretty good when I took a financial class and heard about tithing. I asked a trusted friend, Paul McCullough, about it. I asked him how he could possibly make it giving that much money away to the church. He said he couldn't make it without giving that money away, and he was giving it to God through the church. Paul explained how we have to put action to our faith if we really want to follow Jesus.

Over the next few weeks this teaching on tithing ate at me all of the time. It was a huge step of faith for me and Brooke, but when we began giving God tripled the size of my business. We were amazed at how our business exploded. I'm now able to hire guys who are going through recovery and get them back into the workforce. Brooke has become a stay-at-home mom and we owe it all to Jesus.

[Gold]

Heaven will be a pure and peaceful place. There will be no pain. I'm excited to go to heaven, because I've been through hell on earth, and it's terrible. I go through my days now walking with God, and it's wonderful. God has given me a life I didn't think was possible. I can only imagine how much more wonderful Heaven will be.

[Final Thoughts]

No matter how bad it is, or how bad it has been, if you put your faith in Jesus, you can overcome anything. While life is sometimes incredibly hard, God can help you survive any storm.

words of [HOPE]

"Then he took his staff in his hand,
chose five smooth stones from the stream, put them in the pouch of his shepherd's bag
and with his sling in his hand, approached the Philistine."
1 Samuel 17:40

We all have giants we battle in life — fear, anxiety, depression, greed, addiction, anger, etc. We can battle these giants using the armor of human effort, or with the weapons of supernatural power.

The story of David and Goliath in 1 Samuel 17 illustrates the strategy.

King Saul viewed the battle horizontally, relying upon military gear. Because David had experienced the faithfulness of the Lord in previous encounters, his confidence was in the Lord...and "five smooth stones".

My challenge to you is to identify the giant you are facing, then ask God to reveal to you a promise from His Word that you can turn into a prayer, like placing a stone in your own sling, and each time that giant seeks to intimidate, control, or destroy you, train your mind to turn to the specific promises of God He has given you. Focus your thoughts on the supremacy and sufficiency of Jesus Christ. Memorize passages such as Philippians 4:8, 2 Corinthians 10:5, and Colossians 3:2.

We can all agree, just as David did, that God is faithful. May we walk in confidence in Him and His promises today.

Don Blackmore

Brooke's Story

[Gray]

My family went to church regularly growing up. We hardly ever missed. My parents taught me and my brother good morals and to be good students. We were a close family, but our faith seemed to be a religious thing we kept in its place on Sundays and Wednesday nights. I enjoyed church and had lots of friends there. We loved going to Bogg Springs church camp every year.

[Red]

The summer I was 12 years old, camp was going great like always. During one of the services I felt something different. God was calling me to go forward. After growing up in church, acknowledging Jesus as my Savior made sense in my mind, but I felt something deeper. In the deepest part of my being, the love of Jesus was so real.

[White]

I went forward with a friend from church, Gena Roldan Hudson, who prayed with me. We were surrounded at the altar by several of my friends, crying and praying. It was a special experience, and I felt different inside.

At Bogg Springs Camp they had a tradition where you rang a bell if you got saved. When I rang that bell it sealed the memory of those moments in my mind.

[Blue]

When I got back home I felt different. The next Sunday at church I went forward to surrender to being baptized. I could hardly speak through the emotions and tears. My pastor knew what I wanted and encouraged me greatly.

The following Sunday night I walked out into the baptistery in front of the whole church. I was very nervous, but excited to be obedient to Jesus. After proclaiming Jesus as my Savior, Pastor Tropp dunked me under the water, then after being raised out of the water, he picked me up and gave me a big hug. I was so happy.

[Green]

Unfortunately, I thought you got saved, baptized, and then just lived your life. I wish I had understood that salvation is a relationship with Jesus that needs to be developed. As I got older I began to make worldly, selfish decisions that led me further away from God. I made lots of bad choices and was very good at being sneaky about my sinful lifestyle.

I had met my future husband, John Ryan, when we were young. He played baseball with my brother. I always thought he was cute. In my late teenage years I began dating a guy who turned out to be a drug dealer. We got pulled over by the police and he quickly convinced me to tell them the weed in his car was mine. The police didn't believe me, but I insisted it was mine, so I got a misdemeanor and sentenced to participate in Narcotics Anonymous. I was reconnected with John Ryan at the age of 20 in a drug court meeting.

I broke up with my drug dealing boyfriend and began dating John Ryan. I got pregnant within a month of dating him. Six weeks after we had our first son together, John Ryan's ex-girlfriend dropped off their three year-old son for us to raise. I was suddenly 21 years old with two kids. I had a lot of resentment. This was a very hard start for our marriage.

For the first 10 years of marriage we were selfish. Our parents kept our kids a lot while we partied as much as we could. We both had anxiety, depression, fear, and financial problems. We were incredibly selfish. It was ugly. John Ryan and I used alcohol and marijuana regularly. We hung out with people who used drugs and led bad lifestyles. Nevertheless, we went to church regularly, but it was an empty existence. I think we went to church simply out of habit from how I was raised.

Our life was a mess. I didn't realize it at the time, but I was a horrible wife. I nagged John Ryan relentlessly and always griped about not having enough. We were active with our kids and would take them to sports separately. Eventually, I stopped using drugs and alcohol. I was too busy being a mom and trying to keep up with my life in nursing school.

John Ryan was still using and running with some bad people. I noticed he began avoiding spending time with me. I got pregnant again and he never wanted to be around. Being pregnant, I was emotional, and I began to confront him. I brought home a drug test and he flipped out. He would run away for long periods of time. Eventually, he admitted he was taking

Adderall and wanted to stop. I thought there was more to it, but I was happy he shared something with me.

He began skipping work and was fired. He got another job but he was not dependable. After I had our next son, he continued disappearing. He would say he was going to the store and would be gone all day. This happened all the time.

Our new baby got sick and I had to be at the hospital with him. I was stressed out, because I couldn't count on John Ryan to take care of our other kids. I found out he dropped them off at school before 6:00 a.m. a few times, before anyone else had arrived. He lied and lied to me over the next year. I was depressed and would cry all the time. I was a nurse working 12 hour shifts and life was hard. I kept praying, "God open his eyes!"

John Ryan began running with a new couple and things got even worse. Stuff began disappearing from our house. Soon my dad, brother, and even strangers were calling me telling me John Ryan had stolen from them. The pressure I was under was building up to almost being unbearable. We had a rent house I had worked hard to keep. I drove by it one afternoon and there was a padlock on it and a sign saying it had been foreclosed on. This was my breaking point.

I went home, locked myself in my room and screamed at God, "Why are you putting all this on me?!" I had been praying "Open his eyes", but now my prayer changed to "Open my eyes". My focus shifted to me. I had always wanted God to heal him, but I realized I had to be healthy to raise our children. In my mind, I decided it was time to end our marriage.

Shortly after this, John Ryan's mom called and told me he had stolen his grandmother's Lexus. The police called asking about him, and I was completely honest with them. I went to my mom's lake house with the kids to get away. Up until this point, I hadn't been open with the kids about their daddy. I finally told them their daddy was sick. They looked at me like they wanted me to fix everything. I felt powerless and had no answers for them. We all loved John Ryan, but he had to change or we would lose him.

When I got home, John Ryan was sitting on the couch. I angrily asked him, "What are you going to do now?! You can't run from this one!" He broke down crying and God answered my prayer. He allowed me to see John Ryan as Jesus did: a broken soul in need of a savior. I could see he would soon be dead if he didn't get help.

He was still resisting going to rehab. A short time later I found a text message about him doing an 8-ball. This was my evidence. I had found needles, burnt spoons, and obvious drug paraphernalia he had lied about being his, but this was undeniable. I confronted him and told him if he didn't agree to return to a rehab program, I would call the police. He raised his hands in surrender and agreed to go.

This was on a Friday. I scrambled trying to find a place who would take him in before he changed his mind and ran. I couldn't find one anywhere. My sister-in-law invited me to church that Sunday. I thought, "This is perfect. God will provide my answer at church this Sunday."

As we entered the church, my sister-in-law told me we could go pray at the altar at any time. I immediately went to pray and immediately I was surrounded by several women. A lady named Chrissy Robinson asked me what I was praying for. Through my tears I answered, "My husband is sick and needs Jesus to heal him. He's made terrible choices." She told me, "Jesus will. You go home and tell Satan to leave your home!" Then they all prayed for me, crying out to Jesus for a miracle.

I didn't get the answer I was looking for at church that day, but I received even more. I went home and proclaimed Jesus was the Lord of our family and Satan wasn't welcome there. A peace filled me. And it's a peace I needed, because I still had to deal with John Ryan, and he was detoxing. He was sweating, mad, screaming, and hostile.

I had a friend at work who I respected. I noticed him talking about Jesus regularly, and he kept Bible verses in his pockets he would share. Desperate, I called him. He said he knew of a place called The Father's House who had a bed for John Ryan. I quickly packed his bag, put his Bible in it, and wrote him a note telling him I believed in him. We loaded up and drove out into the middle of nowhere. When we arrived they asked him to write down all of the drugs he was using, so they could help with his detox. I was shocked by how long his list of drugs was.

I thought it would be traumatic dropping him off, but it was just the opposite. I was all cried out. I knew he was at a safe place, and I was at peace. It was the most peaceful I had been in years. The kids said they felt the same way when we talked over the next few days. Although I had decided to divorce John Ryan, God never gave me peace about that decision.

On our first visit, John Ryan tried to leave. I told him if he did I would immediately file for divorce and he would never see the kids again. Thankfully it worked and he stayed. I noticed over the next few weeks a vast difference in my friends. The ones who would share scripture and hope with me were refreshing. Others told me to take care of myself and move on. I wasn't opposed to moving on if it was God's will, but they spoke from worldly feelings, not Biblical advice. There was an obvious difference in their spirits to me. I made some major changes in my friendships during this time. I was constantly in the Bible and John Ryan was too.

When we started really living for Jesus, it changed everything. John Ryan has become my best friend. He is my biggest supporter. He loves our family Big! And as bad as it was, if I had to do it all over again, I would. (But I sure wouldn't want to!)

While I could blame John Ryan for all of our family problems, I know we were both guilty to some extent. It's when we put Jesus first in our marriage that everything changed. Today, John Ryan has his own business and I'm a stay-at-home mom. He uses his successful business to employ people who are recovering from substance abuse. God answered all my prayers, although He answered them in ways I would have never imagined.

[Gold]

I feel like I should be more heavenly minded. Heaven is our hope! The Bible says we are made in the image of God, and I think we will be more like God when we get to heaven. I think heaven will be warm and sunny. Sometimes when I get into deep prayer I feel the presence of God. I think we'll feel that way in heaven all the time.

[Final Thoughts]

You don't have to be perfect for God to love you or use you. He can make the most incredible things out of the ugliest situations. He brings beauty from ashes.

words of [WISDOM]

"You can look forward with hope, because one day there will be no more separation, no more scars, and no more suffering in My Father's House. It's the home of your dreams!"
- Anne Graham Lotz

"Do not be misled:
"Bad company corrupts good character."
- Paul the Apostle
1 Corinthians 15:33

"Whether you think you can or you think you can't, you're right."
- Henry Ford

Maryrose's Story

[Gray]

I was born in Florida, where my father worked for NASA. My parents were originally from Queens, New York and kept a thick accent even when they moved to a new area. My dad loved us and was a good dad, but he was very secretive about his job. My mom, on the other hand, was very outgoing. When I was one, my dad took a new position in Dallas, Texas. They were devout Catholics and we were raised in the Catholic Church. My parents provided everything my siblings and I needed, made sure we were good students, and paid for us to go to college.

I was generally a good girl up until I was 21 years old. I had watched my oldest brother get addicted to drugs and how hard it was on him. When dad found out my brother was abusing drugs, he told him he was going to summer camp, then promptly dropped him off at a rehab facility. Summer camp was a lot different for him that year! It was difficult and took time, but he eventually got clean. He acknowledged Jesus as his Savior and now runs a rehab program himself.

I was studying opera in college and met a gal who worked at the local radio station, and she said they were looking for a DJ. They hired me! After graduating, I decided to pursue a career in radio. I started out doing part-time on the weekends at a very small station. I would drive from Dallas to Tyler Texas every weekend for four years, until I finally got a break on the air in Dallas, my first major market. They offered me an overnight position, and I loved the industry. During this time, I began to make bad decisions, becoming sexually active for the first time.

Unfortunately, during this time, I hurt my back and had to have two spinal surgeries. This is where things really got off track for me. After my surgery, I was given Vicodin and I loved the high it gave me. I continued using it long after I should have stopped. However, I was smart enough to avoid using OxyContin when it was offered to me. I honestly felt like if I tried it, I would end up overdosing and dying from it. I believe God protected me from ever touching it.

From 1994-2005, I abused Vicodin mixing it with alcohol. I never was an alcoholic, but combining the two drugs helped enhance the effect. I worked in radio the whole time I was using.

Although I was raised in a loving, healthy environment, I didn't feel like I deserved to be loved. There wasn't any reason I should have felt this way. Satan uses drugs to enhance the lies he tells you. Drugs helped mask the physical and emotional pain I was going through.

[Red]

In 1998, my oldest brother invited me to a church service. He was now a follower of Jesus and I'm sure he was praying for me. I agreed to go, because I knew it would make him happy.

During the church service, a strange feeling came over me. Church had always been a very strict, religious ceremony in my past. It wasn't ever explained to me as a personal relationship with Jesus. But during this service, Jesus seemed more real than I had ever experienced. It was as if he was speaking to my heart.

[White]

I realized I was a sinner in need of a savior. Jesus opened my eyes to my need for him. I understood God's grace was a gift and not something I could ever earn. I prayed for salvation and believed Jesus was the son of God who died in my place for my sin. It was a special moment, and I wanted to be baptized.

[Blue]

I got baptized a short time later. The pastor of that church, my brother, and his family were there. I remember it meant a lot to me. My brother was also very excited and happy about my decision.

Unfortunately, I didn't have much of an understanding of how to have a relationship with Jesus. I wasn't discipled, and I quickly slipped back into the bad decisions I had been making.

[Green]

I was overweight and decided to have weight loss surgery. I was still using drugs, and after this surgery I ramped up my drug use. I was a mess.

My mom got sick in late 2004. She was prescribed hydrocodone liquid. I'm embarrassed to say I would drink her hydrocodone and fill it back up with water.

I was dating a really nice guy who said I seemed like a good person, but he was worried I was on drugs. He wouldn't continue dating me. I thought I was hiding it and doing fine, but this was a wake-up call.

I realized I needed help at this point. My siblings were very mad at me and one threatened to cut me off from the family. It was a very hard step, but I forced myself to check into rehab. On April 24th, 2005, I began my sobriety. It was a difficult time of self-reflection and discovery, but I came out a better person. I then went to 90 straight days of AA. I was connected with an amazing sponsor who helped me more than words can express.

I apologized to my mom when I got out of rehab. About five weeks later, she called the whole family together. She announced, in no uncertain terms, that she had forgiven me, and my siblings should as well. It meant a lot to me to have my mom's forgiveness.

My family celebrated my sobriety. They were genuinely happy for me. In August of the same year, my mom took a turn for the worse. I went to stay with her in the hospital. I knew she was near the end. I crawled into bed with her and wrapped my arms around her, just like I had done when I was a little girl. I lovingly told her I was healthy now, and I would take care of daddy. She could rest and be with Jesus. Mom took one more breath, and she went to her heavenly home.

I kept my promise. I would visit daddy almost every day, taking care of feeding and bathing him. He had always been so secretive and quiet. This was a special time for us to really enjoy and get to know one another. I'm thankful for that time I had with him. He passed a year and a half later.

In 2008, my oldest brother bought me a "Recovery Bible." My daily religious routine was to say The Rosary, as I had done my whole life, and read my new Bible. Over time, I began to feel God was telling me to stop saying The Rosary and to start praying directly to Jesus. I realized Mary was not a god, and God is a jealous God, he wants a direct relationship with me. The only way to God is through his son, Jesus Christ. Mary was just a regular person God blessed to bring Jesus into the world. It was a life-changing moment. I understood now that I had a personal relationship with God and He loved and cared for me. I kept reading my Bible, but the teachings became much more personal. It was like reading a love letter written especially for me.

Unfortunately, we live in a world where bad things happen. Three months after my life-changing revelation about my relationship with Jesus,

I lost my dream job. Things were going so good in my life and this was a devastating blow. I lost my car and had to get a cheaper one, but through prayer and my sponsor's help, I stayed clean!

A short time later I got another job at an AM radio station. This seemed like an answer to prayer, but my new boss turned out to be not a very nice person to work for. I worked with two other women who he treated just as bad. We became very good friends through this horrible job situation, and they are my sisters for life!

As I continued to grow closer to God, I felt led to give up sex outside of marriage. I didn't decide this lightly, and I committed to stay celibate until I got married. It didn't take long to discover it's difficult to get dates when you announce you're celibate outside of marriage, even with guys who identify as Christians. I had many one and done dates over the next several months.

I noticed a friend of mine named Curtis, who I went to elementary school with, was "liking" many of my social media posts. We messaged back and forth a few times and he asked if he could call me. I agreed. Over the next three hours Curtis told me his messed up life story. It didn't bother me, and I enjoyed the conversation. He asked if we could talk again the next day. I explained to him I was a Christian, and I was choosing to follow the teachings of Jesus, including to be celibate until marriage. He said he was fine with that, so I agreed to talk again. I didn't expect him to call back, but he did!

We began talking regularly and he eventually came to visit me. I knew God had placed him in my life. While we dated, we did a lot of conference calls with my sponsor. I wanted everything on the table and to do things God's way for a change.

One of the most precious items my mom left for me was her 1958 engagement and wedding rings. Six months after reconnecting on Facebook, Curtis took me to the Dallas Cowboys AT&T Stadium, and on the 50-yard line he dropped down to one knee. He pulled out my mom's wedding ring that he had resized and asked me to marry him. Through tears I said, "Yes!" It was 11-12-13. Curtis said we would never forget the date!

We were married the next month. Curtis and I actually attended a "we're getting married class" at our church the month after our wedding! We figured we could use the knowledge and advice.

In our conversations we discovered an ironic story. Curtis had served in the Navy during the Persian Gulf War. His battleship was the first one to arrive in the region at the beginning of the conflict. As they patrolled off the coast, an incoming SCUD missile warning went off. The soldiers braced for impact. It was an explosion that never came, because the bomb was intercepted. The Patriot Missile Defense System saved my future husband's life. It was a system developed by the team my dad had worked on. My daddy had helped save my future husband's life for me.

In 2014, the not so nice station manager at the AM station pushed things too far. Curtis told me to quit. It was hard, because I loved radio, but I turned in my notice. I was learning to trust God to provide.

I went to visit a friend who was working at the number one Christian radio station in the country. She gave me a tour of the station. I realized a guy who I had worked with years before, who had known me during my addiction years, was working there in the programming department. During my tour I asked to see him. I wanted to make amends to him for my behavior from way back then. He accepted my apology, but told me it wasn't necessary. He was glad to hear I had gotten healthy.

About four months later, he messaged me. He asked if I wanted to come and join the air staff part time. I said, "Absolutely!"

Although he had seen me at my worst, he showed me grace. Four years later, he put me on full-time and I promised to make my time slot the #1 listened show. Laughing, he told me being the top slot in any time frame on a Christian station was unlikely. He was wrong! God blessed me in some incredible ways, and my show became the most listened to in any category in my time slot. With God all things are possible! I'm still in Christian radio and love sharing the hope I've found in Jesus daily with multitudes of people.

[Gold]

In heaven, I'm most excited about getting a big 'ol hug from Jesus! I believe heaven will be more beautiful than a Hawaiian beach, the Swiss Alps, or anywhere else here on earth. It's exciting to imagine how wonderful it will be to have Jesus welcoming me to heaven.

[Final Thoughts]

It doesn't matter who you are, where you are, what you do, how much you weigh, or how much money you have or don't have. God loves you right where you are. Call out to Him today and be saved!

words of [HOPE]

"For I know the plans I have for you," declares the LORD,
"plans to prosper you and not to harm you, plans to give you hope and a future."
Jeremiah 29:11

Years ago, prior to knowing the depth of my daughter's struggles, I gave her a framed picture of Jeremiah 29:11. I had no idea the impact of the promise within it God would give to her, and to me. I was a mom whose heart was heavy for her child, not knowing the details but feeling the darkness that surrounded her. I turned to the One who knows all and prayed.

Many tears and prayers led me to the realization that though my love for my daughter was great, God's was greater, and she was more His child than mine. In my heart and soul, I released her into His arms. In that moment, I felt such a peace that God was going to take care of her and never leave her. The change in her wasn't immediate, but I rested in God's assurance. As promised, the day came when I watched the darkness fade. Her eyes began to sparkle again with life, the smile on her face became real, and His plans became her plans.

Don't give up, keep the faith, and you will see the One who holds all of our tomorrows keep His promises.

Kathy Fogarty

James' Story

[Gray]

I was born at Ramey Air Force Base in San Juan, Puerto Rico to Master Tech Sergeant Jerald Richard Loy and homemaker, Addie Mae Brown Loy. My Childhood memories are of a loving home and being in church.

When I was seven, my father was a deacon in a small Baptist church in Anchorage/Fairbanks, Alaska where we were stationed. While living there he was diagnosed with cancer. He passed away one year later, at the age of 31. I was devastated. I felt abandoned, lonely, angry, confused, and was deeply hurt. I couldn't imagine what my life would be like without my dad.

My mother, sister, and I moved to Conway, Arkansas to begin our new life. My mother began working at the University of Central Arkansas administration building, and we attended First Baptist Church in Conway. To gain acceptance, I excelled in academics and athletics. I longed for my father and wanted a male role model to take interest and invest in my life.

I was 14 when my mother was diagnosed with lymphoma. I couldn't understand how a loving God could allow this to happen to His children. Negotiating with Him, I promised to serve Him if He saved my mother and to never believe in Him if He didn't. The next years were extremely difficult as I watched the cancer destroy my young Christian mother's body. But her spirit remained steadfast through it all. She kept a crocheted pillow with the words from 2 Corinthians 12:9 on it, "My grace is sufficient for thee, my strength is perfected in weakness." She continually encouraged me and testified to God's goodness, but I was bitter and angry toward the Lord. After her death I was true to my promise and left God in search of what I wanted in life.

I graduated with honors from Conway High School and worked full time to put myself through college at the University of Central Arkansas. I graduated in four years with a B.B.A. in Marketing in 1987.

In college, I began drinking for the first time in my life, and I lived selfishly. I bought into the world's ideas of what was significant — career, money, and possessions. I obtained two homes, cars, money in the bank, material possessions, and an engagement to my college sweetheart.

I had obtained everything the world said would make me happy, yet I was empty inside. My drinking led to harder experiments with pot, pills, and cocaine. Cocaine became my master, as I made choices that put me in bondage. My cocaine addiction made me realize the old saying about sin is true: It took me farther than I wanted to go, kept me longer than I wanted to stay, and cost me more than I wanted to pay. Never wanting to accept responsibility for my actions, I blamed God.

I eventually had 47 felonies and multiple misdemeanors over the next couple of decades. I lost everything — well over a million dollars — and decided to try to set myself free without the help of God. I tried rehab programs and 12-step programs without success. This time in my life taught me that addiction has only three outcomes: sobered up, locked up, or covered up.

[Red]

I was arrested again. I spent 23 hours a day locked in a jail cell for the next 33 days. This gave me lots of time to think. My mind was drawn back to considering God. Finally, my sister bailed me out. She invited me to attend a Celebrate Recovery service at her church. I agreed to go. I later found out the leaders there, as well as my sister, had been praying for me for the past 23 years.

They helped me connect with a rehab program called John 3:16 Ministries. I called Bryan and Beverly Tuggle at John 3:16 Ministries in June 2005. Bryan said they would love me and try to meet my needs. He stated there would be no cost for the program, because Jesus had already paid the price. That was a good thing, because I didn't have any money left.

I told Bryan I was considering rededicating my life to Christ. He paused and then asked me, "James, I want you to think about this: Can you rededicate something you've never dedicated?"

[White]

It would be two weeks before I could get to the John 3:16 campus. Over those two weeks I thought a lot about Bryan's question. Had I ever really submitted my life to Jesus? There was absolutely no evidence I could think of to support that I had ever really known or followed Jesus.

I arrived at the John 3:16 Ministry campus still filled with anger toward God, but questioning my feelings. The guys there loved me unconditionally. Knowing they had been in my shoes and were fighting to stay clean themselves helped me listen to them.

We had Bible study and classes daily and chapel on Sundays. During my third week there, during a chapel service, God overwhelmed me. I was empty and broken. I went to the altar and cried out to Jesus, from the very depths of my soul, to save me. All my burdens, anger, and hatred were released and I was set free. It felt like a million pounds was lifted off of me. I had known *about* God growing up, but I had never really *known* God. There at that altar, I was changed and made new!

[Blue]

After graduating from the program, I joined West Baptist Church in Batesville. The pastor there, Bob Dailey, discipled me and helped me keep growing in my walk with Jesus. He taught me about the importance and significance of being baptized after we are saved. He explained how baptism is symbolically being buried to our old self and being raised to live a new life in Jesus. I was excited to follow the example Jesus gave us. I cherish the memory of that special day of baptism. I was happy to publicly proclaim Jesus as my Lord.

[Green]

Romans 12:2a says, "Do not be conformed to the pattern of this world, but be transformed by the renewing of your mind." Spending time daily in the Bible renewed my mind. It taught me wisdom and gave me understanding. I learned who I am in Christ, not who the world tells me I am. I also learned about the full armor of God and how to fight spiritual battles. Christianity isn't for the weak but for powerful warriors under God's control.

John 3:16 ministries loved me when I didn't love myself, met my needs abundantly, built my faith, and allowed me the opportunity to develop a personal relationship with Jesus Christ. John 3:16 Ministries is a unique place where God's Holy Spirit moves in a tremendous way. They teach the men who go there how to serve as Jesus did. My time there will always hold a special place in my heart for the opportunity extended to me. Two other members of my family also attended recovery there after my graduation. The impact of this ministry has changed my entire family.

God soon blessed me with my beautiful wife and my two stepsons. I met my wife, Laura, at West Baptist Church in Batesville and we were married January 13, 2007 on the grounds of John 3:16 Ministries.

Jesus Christ is why I am free today. He gives me a peace and joy I have never known. God is the head of my life, my family, and our home. I am a new creation. The old James is gone.

I learned through the "Experiencing God" study that our purpose is knowing God's will and doing His work. I wanted to obey Jesus in helping others find and follow Him. Feeling led to take another step of faith, I was ordained into the ministry at Mt. Zion Baptist Church in Batesville, Arkansas on August 23, 2009.

I began to realize God was calling me to use my experiences, good and bad, to help others. The Lord called me to be the Executive Director of a new recovery facility. The Renewal Ranch program was just being developed when I came onboard. Renewal Ranch's mantra of "Restoring Broken Lives Through Christ" fit perfectly into my purpose in this life.

I was blessed to have my wife, Laura, and our family be united to serve in this calling. We accepted the offer and moved to Conway on August 1, 2009 with the attitude of 'Here I am Lord, send me'.

Having been freed from the bondage of addiction myself, I wanted others to know the freedom found in Jesus Christ. I wanted them to experience His love, peace, joy, contentment, and the freedom He provides. God placed it on my heart to help men trapped in addiction have the opportunity to overcome their struggles at no monetary cost to them. They can learn to serve God, family, and community. They can live an abundant, victorious life. I was so excited for this opportunity and to see and be a part of what God is doing.

The Renewal Ranch ministry purchased 90 acres in May 2010 and started construction on our first lodge. In January 2011 we opened the doors to 8 men. Since that time we have seen over 300 men come to know Jesus Christ as their Lord and Savior. Countless family members have also been saved. We currently have over 300 graduates of the Renewal Ranch Program. Jesus is the only hope we have. Jesus is still in the miracle business. Jesus still redeems, restores, transforms, delivers, and is mighty to save. I am humbled and grateful to be a part of God's story in the lives of so many men and their families.

Luke 12:48 says, "To whom much is given, much will be required." I should be dead or in prison, but by the grace of God I'm alive and free. He had a different plan for my life. God has had me on a rocket ship of restoration these past 15 years and has restored every aspect of life that I destroyed. I want to make an eternal difference with the time I have left. Serving others and sharing the good news of the Lord Jesus Christ is my heart's desire. I want to make disciples that make disciples.

[Gold]

Heaven will be wonderful because we will be with Jesus. I think the defeat of sickness, pain, and suffering will be amazing. I can't wait to worship my Lord, Jesus Christ, face to face. Actually, I'll probably be on my face!

[Final Thoughts]

Jesus is waiting. All you must do is seek Him and you will find Him. I thank God for His grace, mercy, forgiveness, and that He is longsuffering with us, wishing none should perish. You will either receive Jesus as your Lord, or you will reject Him. I pray you choose life in Christ today.

words of [WISDOM]

Among those who self-identified as needing treatment but did not receive it, cost was the biggest barrier.[5]

"Though no one can go back and make a new beginning, anyone can start now and make a brand new ending."
- Carl Bard

The availability of prescription painkillers peaked in 2012 at 81 prescriptions per 100 people. Recent efforts to curtail over-prescription have brought that down to 59 prescriptions per 100 people as of 2017.[5]

Bill's Story

[Gray]
My mom and dad were good parents, and we went to church regularly. As I got older, I noticed that about twice a year my dad would go away for three or four days. Mom would say he was working, but she seemed very emotional and upset while he was away. When I was about 10 years old, my mom told me the truth. My dad was an alcoholic, and he would disappear because he was on a drinking binge. He was my hero. I was crushed and embarrassed.

We continued to go to church, and I accepted my dad's struggles. It wasn't easy, but I did my best to hide my disappointment. For the most part, he hid his alcoholism well.

[Red]
I understood what the church taught about Jesus at an early age. I had heard lessons about how He came to earth to be the perfect sacrifice for our sin since I was a little child. They taught us John 3:16, "For God so loved the world that He gave His only begotten Son, that whoever believes in Him shall not perish, but have eternal life," along with many other Bible verses. It made sense to me.

When I was 12 years old, during a Sunday morning service at Immanuel Baptist Church, I decided it was time for me to become a Christian. I listened to the sermon and felt like this is what Jesus wanted me to do. It wasn't an emotional experience at all.

[White]
When the pastor gave the invitation to come forward I got up and walked to the front. I think it surprised my mom and dad, because I hadn't told them what I was doing. When I got to the front, an adult asked me what I needed. I told them I wanted Jesus to save me from my sins and to become a Christian. We knelt down at the altar, and they prayed with me for salvation.

111

[Blue]

When we got home I had a conversation with my parents about what salvation meant, and they made sure I understood what I was doing. Then we discussed baptism and what it was all about. They were satisfied with my understanding and set up an appointment to visit with our pastor about me being baptized.

When I met with my pastor, he asked me several questions and explained a lot of things about baptism from the Bible to me. After we talked, he set up a time for me to be baptized. I felt good about doing what I was supposed to do.

I had never been nervous about speaking or being in front of anyone, and this didn't bother me either. I remember the water was extremely cold and my parents were proud of me. I was glad to be known as a Christian.

[Green]

My dad got sick when I was in junior high. He was diagnosed with Alzheimer's disease. We slowly stopped going to church. Without the leadership of my dad, my mom and I drifted. I felt cheated, because dad got sick right when I really needed him. I knew it wasn't his fault, but it didn't change the way I felt.

As I drifted away from God, I began to embrace the pleasures of the world. In high school I began drinking beer, smoking pot, and driving a motorcycle. In my mind, I was about as cool as you could get. I lived to party.

I never got arrested, but I just coasted through life. I made it through one semester of college but couldn't afford to continue. I got a job building customized Harley Davidson's. It was a cool job, but it didn't pay well. After a while I was tired of being broke. I ended up getting a free ride to Pulaski Vo-Tech School in their machine shop program. I worked and studied hard, but I didn't mind it because I was enjoying what I was doing. My instructor liked my work ethic and invested a lot of extra time in me.

When I graduated I got a good paying job on the night shift as a machinist. I met a girl and we hit it off. A short time later we got married. We had both partied a lot and were ready to settle down. Early in our marriage we realized something was missing from our life and decided to go back to church. We enjoyed getting back into church and built some good friendships there.

I was visiting a couple's home from our Sunday school class and noticed he had two brand new Mercedes-Benz vehicles in his garage. I asked him what he did for a living. He said he was an investment banker. I told him I wanted to be an investment banker. He just laughed. The next day I called every investment banking company in the phonebook and found one who would interview me. They said if I could pass the test they would hire me. I studied on my own and on my second attempt passed the test.

My wife was upset when I quit my very safe and steady job as a machinist to take a job making only straight commission. If I didn't sell, I wouldn't get paid. But it wasn't long before I was making six figures, and she was happy with my decision.

We had a little girl, Lauren, and then two years later had our son, Alex. Lauren was socially outgoing like me. Alex was more of an introvert like his mom.

My run as an investment banker came to an abrupt end with the 1980's savings and loans collapse. One year I earned over $300,000 and the next I only made $10,000. It wasn't long before my wife and I got divorced. We began with joint custody, but I ended up with full custody. I went from being a rich, successful husband to being a single parent struggling to make it.

I embraced the challenge and tried to be the best dad that I could be. We got a trailer to live in, but it didn't have any furniture. I'm sure this was hard on the kids, but they seemed to handle it well. I kept them in church, and we made the best of those lean years.

When Alex was 12 years old we were attending First Southern Baptist Church in Bryant. He enjoyed the youth group there. He got saved and was soon baptized. I was very proud of him, because going up in front of everyone wasn't easy for him.

Alex enjoyed camping and playing video games, but his favorite thing was going to the movies. We would usually go see one every Friday night. It became "our thing" to do together. He especially liked anything with Batman or Star Wars involved.

Alex was a good kid and rarely ever got into trouble. It was out of character when I caught him smoking pot. I had a talk with him about it and how dangerous drugs can be. It wasn't an issue again until about a year later.

Alex told me he was going to the movies with one of his friends. I told him goodbye and that I loved him, and he left for the evening. The next morning I went to his room to wake him up. As I entered his bedroom I noticed his arms were crossed over his body in a weird way. When I grabbed his arm to wake him, it was cold and stiff. I jumped back screaming! I crawled out of the house crying and screaming. The neighbors came outside to see what was going on. They called 911. I couldn't go back inside to see him, because I knew he was gone. I was in shock.

Most of the next week was a blur. Alex's friend, who he had gone to the movies with, told me he had taken methadone. He said it was only the second time Alex had ever taken it or any drugs other than weed. My church friends from Geyer Springs Baptist Church and First Southern Baptist Church surrounded me with love. When I found out it would be $8,000 for the funeral I was at a loss. I didn't have it. A church friend found out about the situation and paid the expenses.

I had been dating a girl named Vicki for about five months. Her husband had died the previous year. Her role in helping me was huge. She was a great support for me during this time, and I needed a lot of support.

I fantasized about tracking down the person who sold Alex the drugs and killing him. This became my obsession for a while. I eventually decided going to prison for murder wouldn't solve my problems or relieve my pain. But my pain was so bad.

One particularly rough day I was hurting so bad, so deep in my chest, I wanted to die. I grabbed my .45 pistol and drove toward the cemetery where Alex was buried. My plan was to say goodbye to him and kill myself. Fortunately, the cemetery was 35 miles away. I had Christian music playing and as I drove, the words of hope and love flowed through my speakers. God brought thoughts of how Vicki and my daughter Lauren would feel if I was gone. By the time I arrived at the cemetery God had given me peace.

A year later, I was happy to pay my friend back for Alex's funeral. Two years after Alex passed away, my friend, Scott Curtis, came by to talk with me at work. He said he knew about my son and told me he thought I should become a Gideon. The Gideon organization's primary activity is distributing copies of the Bible free of charge. The Bibles in hotel rooms are usually provided by the Gideon's.

I asked him why he thought I should become a Gideon. He said they went to a detention center occasionally and Alex's story would go a long way with the 50-60 boys who were in there. I had never shared Alex's story, but I felt like God wanted me to do this, so I agreed.

The first time I shared Alex's story I felt unqualified to speak to people about Jesus. I said, "Lord, tell me what to say." The Lord gave me the words to speak and 17 kids came down to pray for salvation that morning. I've learned that God can use our deepest hurts for good if we allow him to.

Today, I'm not angry. I'm not bitter. I trust God. Vicki and I are happily married. Lauren is a nurse practitioner. I have Alex's birth, baptism, and death certificates on my desk. His baptism certificate means the most to me.

[Gold]

It is wonderful to know my mom, dad, and son are all in heaven together. All your troubles, worries, fears will be gone there. Heaven will be more fantastic and perfect than we can imagine.

[Final Thoughts]

God can get you through anything. Lean into Him. Never give up! Never. Ever. Give. Up.

words of [WISDOM]

Fentanyl, a pain medication that is nearly 100 times stronger than morphine, stands out for an 800% increase in overdose deaths in just four years. Even tiny doses of Fentanyl can be deadly. [6]

"Character cannot be developed in ease and quiet. Only through experience of trial and suffering can the soul be strengthened, ambition inspired, and success achieved."
- Helen Keller

"I can do all things through Him who strengthens me."
- Paul the Apostle
Philippians 4:13

Christina's Story

[Gray]

I was born to a mother addicted to drugs and alcohol and a father in the military. At two weeks old, my mother laid me on the bed and wandered off to get high. Days later my dad came home to find me there alone. My dad rushed me to the hospital where I spent the first several months of my life.

When I turned two years old, my dad put me up for adoption. He was too busy with the military to take care of me. A family, who already had four children, adopted me. All of their kids were much older than me, so I felt like an only child. My new family was very religious. Mom drove the church bus and we were there every time the doors were open. I understood at an early age the only way to get to heaven was through faith in Jesus.

[Red]

When I was 11 years old, I went to summer church camp. During one of the services I experienced a feeling I had never felt before. I knew it was God, and although I had been in church all my life, I was fighting Him. I don't know why, because I believed God was loving and kind. For some reason, when I faced my sin, it was distressing, even frightening.

[White]

Immediately after the service, I went and found the pastor. I told him I felt like if I died I would go to hell. He was very loving and kind. We discussed my understanding of God, sin, heaven and forgiveness. I prayed, acknowledging Jesus as my Lord and Savior. All my fears were put to rest. God's love was amazing.

[Blue]

About three months later, I was excited to get baptized. It was the day before my birthday in January. My pastor warned me the heater in the baptistery had broken. It was freezing. Still I was happy about being publicly baptized and symbolically having my sins washed away.

[Green]

My relationship with Jesus grew deeper over the next couple of years. I remained active in church, and one of our female youth leaders was like a best friend to me. I couldn't imagine life without my church and God in it.

As I grew older, I began to grow jealous of all the time my parents spent ministering to others. They were always busy helping other people and not investing time in our relationship. A much older guy in our church began showing me the attention I craved. At the age of 15, I got pregnant. It was a shock to my parents and our church. Already embarrassed and scared, I was not shown any grace. During a Sunday morning sermon, our pastor used me as an example of how not to live. This crushed me.

We got married and kept going to church, but after being so hurt I wasn't engaged at all. A short time later, my husband became abusive. I discovered he had begun using crack cocaine. Having never been around drugs I was in shock.

We divorced, and at 18 years old my life wasn't anything like I had imagined it would be. A single, lonely, divorced, single parent wasn't something I ever dreamed I would become.

I met another man who had been raised totally different than me. He had never gone to church and was raised in a broken, alcoholic home. He drank and smoked weed, but he was good to me and my child. I decided I could change him into the husband and father we needed.

He agreed to go to church, and I dabbled in drinking and drugs to meet him in the middle. He got saved and we got married. Over the next 14 years, we became what I had envisioned. We went to church, on mission trips, and added more kids to our family.

Then one day, out of nowhere, the bottom dropped out. He began drinking heavily and cheating on me. During this time, I got a call from my half-sister — who I had found — saying she knew where my biological mom was, and that she was dying. Deep down I had always desired to meet her and get some closure on why she didn't want me.

We went to my biological mom's home and I was introduced as my half-sister's friend. My mom looked really bad. I found out her criminal rap sheet was 22 pages long and drugs had ravished her body. Eventually my half-sister revealed to my mom that I was her daughter and left the room. My mom was remorseful and told me she had tried to locate me. But as we talked, she got extremely defensive and ended up angrily telling me if I didn't like how she had handled things, I could leave. I left still feeling like a failure, because I wasn't good enough for her. This broke my heart and I sank into deep depression.

When I got back home, my husband tried to restore our marriage, but I didn't care. Eventually, we got divorced. My alcoholism increased significantly after our divorce. I got two DWI's and lost custody of my children to their father who now lived in Alaska. I wanted a fresh start, so I put a map on the wall and threw a dart which landed on Boston, Massachusetts.

I landed a high paying job there and continued in my alcoholism. I got another DWI, but they never found out about my previous others. I got probation. My adopted mom fell ill during this time and passed away. I felt horrible for not being there to say goodbye. When I heard my adopted dad was sick, I left Boston and moved back to be near him.

I met a new guy there and noticed abusive tendencies in him. He had a child, and although I barely knew him, I was drawn to try to help him and his child. My tendency to try and fix other people was turning out to be a bad trait. He threw me against a wall and I called the police. He was arrested. He was already on probation, so when he failed the drug test they administered, his charges increased exponentially.

He convinced me it was my fault. We had only known each other for three months, but to help keep him from going to prison, I married a man I didn't love. A short time later I found out he was dealing a large amount of drugs out of our house. This was a major drug ring. I began drinking a gallon of vodka a day just to cope. I was terrified for my life.

While drunk one day, a friend of his shot me up with meth. I immediately gave up drinking and became a meth addict. Meth gave me energy to function. I embraced the drug culture and began making drug runs for him.

My son came to visit us with his girlfriend. It was great to see him. A few days into his visit, I found him doing drugs in my home. I was devastated. I sent him back to his hometown.

Shortly after this I became deathly ill. I was med-flighted to a major hospital. Once I recovered I decided to get clean. Three months into my recovery, I relapsed. This led to me stealing a drug dealer's car and being a passenger in a high-speed car chase. The driver ditched the car with me in it, and I was suddenly surrounded by police, guns, and dogs. The stolen car was full of guns and drugs. I was arrested facing 14 felony counts.

After two weeks in jail, I was released to await trial. I got permission to move to California where I entered a 12-step program and lived sober for about 9 months.

The time for my trial came up. I traveled back to the state where I was arrested to face my sentencing. I was able to get the sentence reduced to 120 days in rehab and 3 years of probation.

During my time in the rehab program we had classes and chapel. One day during chapel, with about 300 other women in there, I felt God speaking to me. He was telling me I was made for more. I broke down sobbing. Then I felt Him say He loved me and wanted me back. I felt God in that moment more than I had in my entire life. I rededicated my life to Him. The rest of my time in rehab was spent digging into the Bible and rediscovering my love for Jesus.

I received a letter from my husband. Although we had been separated for some time, he told me he was now following God and we were still married. He wanted me to come home. When I was released I had nowhere else to go, so I went back to him thinking we were on the same page. We weren't.

Two weeks after getting home, I woke up to him trying to kill me. He was stomping on me with his boots. I was placed in a women's shelter after getting out of the hospital. A week later they allowed me to go get my stuff from his house. When I walked in, he was there! They had released him from jail without informing the women's shelter.

He attacked me again this time choking me until I passed out. He had the audacity to call the police and tell them I had broken into his house. Fortunately, he was arrested again.

I held on to my faith in Jesus this time! I stayed sober and dealt with the pain. I received a letter from the state parole board where I had been arrested saying I had broken my probation. I knew I hadn't, so I wasn't too worried. My lawyer fought this for a year. I maintained my walk with God, but was unexpectedly arrested and sent back to face my supposed probation violation.

This time in jail was different. I wasn't guilty, and God gave me peace. I spent my time ministering to others. A lady from the facility visited me one day and told me God had revealed to her that I was there to save my life. I didn't understand it at the time. I found out later, while I was locked up, that the man who had tried to kill me twice had been released from prison early and was looking for me to kill me. If I hadn't been locked up, he very well may have been successful this time.

I got released and exonerated from breaking parole. The season I spent in jail wasn't wasted. I used it to develop a stronger relationship with God.

God has moved me to a new city and brought a godly man into my life. We love to serve Jesus together. I'm amazed at the grace Jesus has shown me. I am now pursuing a counseling degree and using my experiences to help others. I take every opportunity I get to proclaim His love and His offer of salvation to all who repent, believe, and follow Jesus!

[Gold]

Heaven will be a place filled with joy and happiness. It will be peaceful. There will be no suffering. I'll be able to see the Son of God who gave away every single part of Himself so I can be there with Him!

[Final Thoughts]

Never give up. Tough times and trials will come, but Jesus is stronger than the temptations. Keep your eyes on Jesus, and do what He wants you to do. His way is best!

words of [WISDOM]

"Recovery is not for people who need it; it's for people who want it."
- Anonymous

"Watch and pray so that you will not fall into temptation. The spirit is willing, but the flesh is weak."
-Jesus Christ
Matthew 26:41

"Success is the sum of small efforts, repeated day in and day out."
- Robert Collier

Nick's Story

[Gray]

I was the sixth of seven kids. My parents also raised their nephew, so we had ten people in our home. Mom was a strict disciplinarian. Dad provided for us, but was passive in his role in guiding our family. I had very low self-esteem growing up. Wearing glasses, hand-me-down clothes, and being poor made me very insecure about who I was as a person. I was bullied a lot and tried not to be noticed.

My parents were very social and every weekend would have a block party. People would come from all around to party with us. This conditioned me to see life as a big party early on. We didn't attend church, but mom was a very generous lady. She would prepare extra food and have us deliver it to neighbors who she knew needed it.

Mom started taking us to church. I noticed the parties slowed down considerably. Everyone but dad would attend church on Sunday. I participated, but didn't really understand what church was really all about.

My dad's job with the railroad moved us from Omaha to Arkansas when I was about 10 years old. This was a major change to my life. I've always been a dreamer. My low self-esteem kept me quiet and made me feel like I had to do everything ten times better than everyone else just to be accepted. Without my father intentionally guiding me into manhood, it was tough to know how to act like a young man.

I remember the first time I had my first sip of alcohol. A relative gave me a few sips when I was 13 years old. It didn't taste great, but it made me lose a lot of my inhibitions. I felt bolder, stronger—less aware of my inadequacies.

At 14 years old I would drink with some friends. At 16 I smoked my first joint. All my life I had been trying to escape from who I was and marijuana helped with that a lot. Deep down I just wanted to be accepted by the crowd.

I began stealing to fit in with people I wanted to be friends with. I got caught a few times. Mom began to write me off. She quit asking me to church, because I never wanted to go anyway. I began dealing drugs.

Just before I turned 17, a guy hit my girlfriend. I went after him and ended up getting arrested for having a gun. I spent the next two weeks locked up in juvenile detention. I was released to home confinement wearing an ankle bracelet.

New Year's Eve rolled around and my sister came to town. I asked my dad if I could go visit her at her hotel. Dad agreed to let me go. At this time I had an older man looking for me, because I owed him money from a drug deal. I ended up cutting off my ankle monitor and skipping town with my sister back to Kansas City.

Three months later I was dealing drugs there. I was drinking heavily, smoking weed, and added sherm (PCP) to the mix. I mostly lived in drug houses moving from one to another constantly.

Over the next seven years, I lived in Kansas City. I had two sons during this time. I also was arrested and put on probation. Part of my sentence was to get a job. I landed a job traveling to neighboring states installing fiber optic cable. This industry was very heavily into drug use, and I increased my use dramatically. I added cocaine which brought out some demons in me.

I was laid off and returned to Kansas City. Although I had made a lot of money, I didn't have any savings. My escape from reality continued to be drugs. One night, I felt like God spoke to me and told me to go back home to Arkansas. I was broke, owed people money, and had no idea how I could get home.

I remembered having visited a church where I was at when I was a teenager with my church youth group. Nasty and stinking, I went there on Sunday. I looked and smelled like the homeless addict I was. They asked me how they could help me. I told them my situation and they bought me a bus ticket home. When I arrived my mom was shocked, but she welcomed me.

I got a job working with a guy in construction. We were working on the home of a beautiful woman. We got to talking and I told her all about myself. Surprisingly she agreed to go on a date with me. She was a church-going Christian and took a big chance on me. I was still a boy in a man's body.

We fell in love and got married. She believed in me and began encouraging me to start my own remodeling business. I was able to get a grant to go to a community college for a construction management degree. During this time, I went ahead and started my own remodeling business like my wife had encouraged me to do. This brought in lots of cash. We invested in seven rent houses. Unfortunately, I hadn't lost my love of drugs. I slowly got back into using. We ended up filing for bankruptcy.

We separated for about six months. I realized I had a problem and began attending Narcotics Anonymous meetings. I actually enjoyed the meetings, and realized I wasn't alone in my struggles. N.A. was good for me, but it didn't solve my fundamental problem: sin.

One morning, I kissed my wife and left for work. On my way to work I craved getting high. I found a dealer and used again. Afterward, I was so disappointed in myself. I disappeared for two weeks, staying high and living in abandoned houses.

[Red]

I came to the end of myself and decided to commit suicide by overdosing. I took an enormous amount of drugs and laid down on the bank of the river. Several hours later, amazingly, I woke up!

I cried out loud to God, "If You are real and have a plan for me, You have to fix me! If you do, I will always live for you!" I went straight to my mom's house and confessed everything. I asked my parents if they would assist me in getting help. My mom had worked with churches who had knowledge of recovery ministries and contacted them. They told her about two programs. John 3:16 ministries was one of them. We contacted them on a Friday. They told me to come to their service on Sunday and apply.

I went, and during the service I cried my eyes out. This place was so beautiful. I knew this is where God could help me. They were full, so I had to come back the next week. My insecurity kicked in, and I didn't think they would ever take me. I didn't feel worthy. On my third visit, I was admitted into the program.

With my cell phone taken, listening to only Christian music, and the drugs getting out of my system, my mind cleared up. I fell in love with Christian music. The lyrics are so deep and powerful. I felt love from the other men there, regardless of their race. I also started feeling life from God inside of my soul.

[White]

Waking up early one morning I felt like a weight lifted off of me, and God filled the void in my heart. I could see a hope and a future. I felt like a new creation — a brand new person. This was my day of salvation!

God blessed me to be in just the right place, at just the right time to draw me to himself. After this experience, I wanted to soak up everything I could about God. I read my Bible with passion and shared with everyone who would listen about the amazing power of God to redeem. I wanted others to have what I had been given.

[Blue]
John 3:16 Ministries sets up a day every so often for people to be baptized. There were about 50 people being baptized with me. The beautiful pond on their grounds was such a fantastic place to experience baptism.

The ceremony of being baptized meant so much to me. I had studied the story of Jesus being baptized by John the Baptist. This story played out in my mind as I went through my actual baptism. It was an incredible experience for me.

[Green]
I graduated from John 3:16 Ministries and went back home to my wife. I did not have a job at the time, so I would find where John 3:16 was serving and go serve with them. I eventually got a job working at an apartment complex in maintenance. I remembered reading in the Bible to ask God for what I wanted, so I asked for a different job where I could learn more. He provided me another job at the arena in my city. Because of this, I was able to help John 3:16 Ministries use this arena free of charge for fundraising events. A few years later, God opened the door for me to work at a local hospital.

I've always loved music. God began using music to allow me to reach others for Him. At first, my sons and I would record music together at the house. A friend of mine started doing gospel music, and invited me to do some Christian hip-hop music with him. I followed that up with a single of my own. My wife and I then started a radio show on a local station.

Influenced by my mom feeding people in our neighborhood growing up, I began feeding the homeless on my own in my spare time. I got a call from a friend who is starting a new recovery program, M-18, in my hometown. He invited me to serve with them. I now teach there regularly.

I share my testimony and the love of Jesus every chance I get. I'm honored to be a deacon at my church. I have a faith based t-shirt company.

My wife and I have a radio show, "Nick and Nita", on Saturday nights. We also have a Facebook live show. And I am filming a visual show for the United Gospel Network my wife will be hosting.

Most recently, I was nominated for two hip-hop artists awards in Atlanta, Georgia. I currently have four songs streaming live. And I have just established a new recording label: Branded Music. As God expands these opportunities, I will follow, and I will always use my platform to point to Jesus.

God took an insecure boy who always tried to hide, and transformed him into a man who loves to share his testimony on TV, radio, social media, and in person. My purpose is to simply share what God has done for me and let you know He can do it for you too!

[Gold]

Heaven will be better than anything we can imagine, and I can imagine a whole lot! There won't be poverty or greed. Everyone will be excited all the time. The best things in this world are simply a taste of how amazing heaven will be. Imagine your very best moment in this life, and know that heaven will be a million times better! There will be incredible praise and worship! It will be off the chain!

[Final Thoughts]

I was chasing so much in this world that I thought would bring me happiness, but when I surrendered to Jesus, He gave me the desires of my heart.

words of [WISDOM]

"The chains of drugs are too weak to be felt until they're too strong for you to break. But Jesus is stronger!"
-Anonymous

"Call on me in the day of trouble;
I shall rescue you, and you will honor me."
Psalm 50:15

"Anyone can give up; it is the easiest thing in the world to do. But to hold it together when everyone would expect you to fall apart, now that is true strength."
- Chris Bradford

A Note to the Reader about Salvation

The grace of God is simply amazing. The stories throughout this book share a wide variety of ways in which Jesus has chosen to work. This life is hard. We yearn for something greater than anything this world has to offer. Our soul will never completely rest until we find our rest in the One who created us. Jesus offers rest and healing for your soul. If you haven't experienced this new life in Jesus, it is available to you right now.

We are all sinners in need of a Savior. The Bible says that every person has sinned (Romans 3:23). It goes on to say, while we don't deserve salvation, God offers it to us as a free gift (Romans 6:23). In fact, while we were enemies of God and living in sin, God sent His only Son to die for us (Romans 5:8). God did this because He loves us so much, and we can receive eternal life with God by believing in His Son, Jesus Christ (John 3:16). We show evidence of this faith in Jesus by believing in our hearts and confessing with our mouths that Jesus is Lord (Romans 10:9-10). The very first thing the Bible teaches us to do once we are saved is to be baptized (Romans 6:4-5). The next step in our relationship is to fellowship with other believers and to grow spiritually.

God loves you no matter how bad you think you are. You are not too far gone for Jesus to save you. Call out to God, turn from the direction you are going, and follow Him. You can do that right now in your own words if you like. If you need someone to talk with or are interested in learning more about what it means to have a relationship with Jesus Christ, a great resource is 1-888-Need-Him (1-888-633-3446). Or on the web, go to www.needhim.org. You can also chat with someone about what a relationship with Jesus is all about at www.chataboutjesus.com. I pray you will acknowledge Jesus as your Lord and receive salvation today!

A Note to those Who Need Help with Substance Abuse

If you are currently struggling with addiction THERE IS HOPE! As you can see through these true stories, if you want help, it is available — but you have to want it. If you want to reach out to speak with someone for help, there are several great biblically based programs.

Many churches and hospitals have substance abuse recovery programs. Teen Challenge is a nationally known program with great results that is not only for teens. Their phone number is 855-363-2334. On the web teenchallengeusa.org. Please don't hesitate to get help.

You are loved more than you know!

Notes

1. Charles Spurgeon's full sermon can be found at www.blueletterbible.org/Comm/spurgeon_charles/sermons/3278.cfm

2. www.drugabuse.gov (updated 2020)

3. From hazeldenbettyford.org (3-13-19)

4. Niaaa.nih.gov (7-10-2020)

5. www.USAfacts.org (5-20-2019)

6. www.USAfacts.org (5-20-2019)

For Other Books by Brad Duncan Visit BooksByBrad.com.

First Fruits and Second Chances follows the story of a pastor who faces a crisis of belief and how God uses this to challenge him, his family and the Church.

The Decision is a story about a popular high school athlete who unexpectedly faces the choice of following Jesus. Two paths lay before him. See how life-altering one decision can be. For Chase Barkley this isn't just another choice, it's The Decision.

Jobe: A story of Grace is available for free. It's a modern day short-story based upon the Old Testament book of the Bible, Job.

Deer Hunter's Devotional 1 and 2 are personal stories from deer hunting Brad has experienced. A practical spiritual thought is attached to each of the 31 fun stories in each book.

Accidental Author is a free ebook sharing the story of Brad's unexpected writing journey.

Colors of Salvation: Substance Abuse is the first book in the Colors of Salvation book series. It shares true life testimonies from a variety of people who have gone through substance abuse, been saved by the amazing grace of Jesus, and are now living boldly for God.

Made in the USA
Coppell, TX
18 January 2021

48417224R00080